# TEA

# Edible

Series Editor: Andrew F. Smith

EDIBLE is a revolutionary series of books dedicated to food and drink that explores the rich history of cuisine. Each book reveals the global history and culture of one type of food or beverage.

Already published

*Apple* Erika Janik, *Avocado* Jeff Miller, *Banana* Lorna Piatti-Farnell, *Barbecue* Jonathan Deutsch and Megan J. Elias, *Beans* Nathalie Rachel Morris, *Beef* Lorna Piatti-Farnell, *Beer* Gavin D. Smith, *Berries* Heather Arndt Anderson, *Biscuits and Cookies* Anastasia Edwards, *Brandy* Becky Sue Epstein, *Bread* William Rubel, *Cabbage* Meg Muckenhoupt, *Cake* Nicola Humble, *Caviar* Nichola Fletcher, *Champagne* Becky Sue Epstein, *Cheese* Andrew Dalby, *Chillies* Heather Arndt Anderson, *Chocolate* Sarah Moss and Alexander Badenoch, *Cocktails* Joseph M. Carlin, *Coffee* Jonathan Morris, *Corn* Michael Owen Jones, *Curry* Colleen Taylor Sen, *Dates* Nawal Nasrallah, *Doughnut* Heather Delancey Hunwick, *Dumplings* Barbara Gallani, *Edible Flowers* Constance L. Kirker and Mary Newman, *Eggs* Diane Toops, *Fats* Michelle Phillipov, *Figs* David C. Sutton, *Foie Gras* Norman Kolpas, *Game* Paula Young Lee, *Gin* Lesley Jacobs Solmonson, *Hamburger* Andrew F. Smith, *Herbs* Gary Allen, *Herring* Kathy Hunt, *Honey* Lucy M. Long, *Hot Dog* Bruce Kraig, *Ice Cream* Laura B. Weiss, *Jam, Jelly and Marmalade* Sarah B. Hood, *Lamb* Brian Yarvin, *Lemon* Toby Sonneman, *Lobster* Elisabeth Townsend, *Melon* Sylvia Lovegren, *Milk* Hannah Velten, *Moonshine* Kevin R. Kosar, *Mushroom* Cynthia D. Bertelsen, *Mustard* Demet Güzey, *Nuts* Ken Albala, *Offal* Nina Edwards, *Olive* Fabrizia Lanza, *Onions and Garlic* Martha Jay, *Oranges* Clarissa Hyman, *Oyster* Carolyn Tillie, *Pancake* Ken Albala, *Pasta and Noodles* Kantha Shelke, *Pickles* Jan Davison, *Pie* Janet Clarkson, *Pineapple* Kaori O'Connor, *Pizza* Carol Helstosky, *Pomegranate* Damien Stone, *Pork* Katharine M. Rogers, *Potato* Andrew F. Smith, *Pudding* Jeri Quinzio, *Rice* Renee Marton, *Rum* Richard Foss, *Saffron* Ramin Ganeshram, *Salad* Judith Weinraub, *Salmon* Nicolaas Mink, *Sandwich* Bee Wilson, *Sauces* Maryann Tebben, *Sausage* Gary Allen, *Seaweed* Kaori O'Connor, *Shrimp* Yvette Florio Lane, *Soup* Janet Clarkson, *Spices* Fred Czarra, *Sugar* Andrew F. Smith, *Sweets and Candy* Laura Mason, *Tea* Helen Saberi, *Tequila* Ian Williams, *Tomato* Clarissa Hyman, *Truffle* Zachary Nowak, *Vanilla* Rosa Abreu-Runkel, *Vodka* Patricia Herlihy, *Water* Ian Miller, *Whiskey* Kevin R. Kosar, *Wine* Marc Millon, *Yoghurt* June Hersh

# Tea

## A Global History

*Helen Saberi*

REAKTION BOOKS

*For Nasir Saberi, with whom I have shared many cups of tea*

*And to the memory of John Canning, my father, who used to bring me an early morning strong cup of tea, and to Alan Davidson, who liked to have a kipper with his tea*

Published by Reaktion Books Ltd
Unit 32, Waterside
44–48 Wharf Road
London N1 7UX, UK
www.reaktionbooks.co.uk

First published 2010
Reprinted 2013, 2016, 2021

Printed and bound in India by Replika Press Pvt. Ltd

British Library Cataloguing in Publication Data

Saberi, Helen
Tea: a global history. – (Edible)
1. Tea. 2. Tea – History.
I. Title II. Series
641.3´384-DC22

ISBN 978 1 86189 776 3

# Contents

Introduction 7

1 What is Tea? 10

2 China 27

3 Japan, Korea and Taiwan 42

4 Caravans and Mediterranean Shores 57

5 Tea Comes to the West 85

6 India, Sri Lanka and Indonesia 125

7 Tea Today and Tomorrow 145

Recipes 148

Glossary 159

References 165

Select Bibliography 168

Websites and Associations 171

Acknowledgements 173

Photo Acknowledgements 174

Index 176

# Introduction

The first cup caresses my dry lips and throat,
The second shatters the walls of my lonely sadness,
The third searches the dry rivulets of my soul to find the stories
of five thousand scrolls.
With the fourth the pain of past injustice vanishes through
my pores.
The fifth purifies my flesh and bone.
With the sixth I am in touch with the immortals.
The seventh gives such pleasure I can hardly bear.
The fresh wind blows through my wings
As I make my way to Penglai.
—*Lu Tong*[1]

The Chinese sip it from tiny cups, the Japanese whisk it. In America they serve it iced. The Tibetans add butter. The Russians serve with lemon. Mint is added in North Africa. Afghans flavour it with cardamom. The Irish and the British drink it by the gallon with milk and sugar. The Indians boil it with condensed milk. In Australia it is brewed in a 'billy' can.

Tea, made from the dried leaves of the evergreen shrub *Camellia sinensis* infused in boiling water, is consumed by millions across the world. It is the second most popular beverage in the world after water. Tea quenches thirst, heals and sustains. It is drunk for enjoyment and for health. Wherever and however it is taken, tea brings well-being, harmony, politeness, conviviality and hospitality. From its legendary beginnings in China to its present-day popularity, tea has had a long and vivid history. Its story is steeped in ritual and religion, adventure and enterprise, smuggling and revolution, literature and social change.

The word tea comes from the Chinese Amoy word *t'e*, pronounced tay. The Dutch, who were the first to import tea into Europe from the port of Amoy in Fujian Province, called it *thee*, which became 'tea' in English. The Mandarin word for tea is *cha*, which became *ch'a* (pronounced tcha) in Cantonese. Variations passed into other languages, becoming *chai* in India, Afghanistan, Persia, Russia and Turkish and *shai* in Arabic. Cha or char was the form in which it first appeared in English in the late sixteenth century and the word still survives colloquially in the expression 'a cup of char'.

At first mainly valued for its health benefits, drinking tea was later discovered by Buddhists to be an effective way of keeping awake during long hours of meditation. The Japanese call tea *O Cha*, meaning honourable tea, and have evolved the elaborate ritual of the tea ceremony. This book describes some of the traditions of tea-drinking and hospitality that have evolved over hundreds of years.

Very early in its history tea was transported along ancient caravan routes and traded in distant and remote regions. We discover how tea came to the West in the days when clipper ships raced to be the first to unload their precious cargoes. We visit tea gardens and tea houses, look at tea dances and see how the great British tradition of afternoon tea began. Across the Atlantic we encounter the famous Boston Tea Party which played a part in America's pursuit of independence; the invention of iced tea and the tea bag; and the latest trends of chai and bubble tea.

We learn how the tea plant was discovered in India and how India has become the second largest producer in the world after China. We observe how tea played an important social role during the Raj; how the people of India drank it in Irani cafes and how it is enjoyed today, when myriad types of tea are produced around the world from Argentina to Zimbabwe. How did all this begin? This book tells the story.

# I
# What is Tea?

In Chinese legend, the story of tea begins with Emperor Shen Nong (2737–2697 BC), also known as the Divine Healer, the Divine Husbandman and the Divine Cultivator. The Emperor decreed that to preserve their health his subjects must boil water before drinking it. One day while he was boiling water some leaves, blown by the wind, accidentally fell into the pot. Tasting the result, Shen was not only delighted with the flavour but also felt invigorated. The leaves came from the plant which we know today as *Camellia sinensis*. Shen ordered extensive planting and recommended the infusion to his subjects, declaring, 'Tea gives vigour to the body, contentment to the mind and determination of purpose.'

The Japanese attribute the beginnings of tea to Dharma (also known as Bodhidharma), a missionary Buddhist monk who travelled from his native India to China at the end of the fifth century. The legend tells how Dharma dedicated seven years to a sleepless devotion to the Buddha. During meditation he found his concentration failing so he cut off his eyelids to stay awake and threw them on the ground. A tea plant grew from each spot where the eye lids had fallen. The leaves of this plant were made into a drink which stimulated the holy man and his flagging worshippers.

Some sources claim that tea originally grew wild in Assam and, according to another legend, the Buddhist scholar Wu Li Zhen, who had been studying in India, returned to China around 53 BC with seven tea plants which he planted on Meng mountain in Sichuan. This story is borne out by the fact that the earliest records of tea being cultivated come from Sichuan at this time. The tea planted on Meng mountain has become famous in China and is known as Gan Lu, meaning 'sweet dew'.

Yunnan also has a long history of tea and there are still many old wild indigenous tea trees there, including one in Bada which is believed to be 1,800 years old. It was from Yunnan that the awareness of tea spread to other parts of China and on to the rest of Asia.

*Camellia sinensis*, Company School, India, 19th century, watercolour.

Whatever the origins of tea, there are many varieties and all come from the same white-flowering evergreen shrub, *Camellia sinensis*. When the wild plant was discovered by the British in Assam in north-eastern India in the early nineteenth century some botanists thought that a new species had been found and named the plant *Thea assamica*. Some people still use this name although it is now generally agreed that all tea comes from *Camellia sinensis*, of which there are three main varieties: China (*C. sinensis* var. *sinensis)*; Assam (*C. sinensis* var. *assamica)*; and Cambodia (*C. sinensis* var. *cambodiensis*. The different varieties produce tea of distinct flavours and qualities.

The China variety is a small-leaved bush with multiple stems which is pruned to a height of one to three metres. The small leaves produce a delicate tea. When allowed to grow wild it can grow to a height of 8 to 20 metres and can live for hundreds of years.

The Assam variety produces tea with a strong earthy flavour. It is a small tree, single-stemmed, with large leaves. In the wild it can reach a height of 6 to 20 metres but on tea estates it is trimmed to just above waist level. The cultivated bush can live for about 40 years.

The Cambodian variety is a hybrid of the Assam and China varieties, taking its flavour and qualities from both.

These three varieties have been cultivated extensively and used to make hybrids, just like grapes for making wine. Also as with wine, the flavour of a particular tea will reflect the climate and soil of the growing environment, thus creating myriad teas with different tastes and flavours.

The young leaves of all these plants are processed into different types of tea. The qualities of a tea reflect the different ways in which it is grown, harvested, handled and dried.

Tea is usually grown between 1,000 and 7,000 feet (300 to 2,000 m) above sea level; tea grown at a higher level usually has a better flavour. Temperature and rainfall are also important. The best temperatures for growing range from 50 to 85°F (10–24°C) and rainfall should be about 80 to 90 inches (200 to 230 cm) a year, although tea can grow well with less rain.

The tea plants are pruned annually to keep them at a medium height, which makes harvesting easier. Plucking the leaves requires quick and nimble fingers and is usually done by women and children. They pick only the bud and a few leaves (usually two) at the end of the shoot.

The method of treating determines the kind of tea produced. There are six types: white, yellow, green, oolong, black and puerh. White, yellow and green teas are 'unfermented'; oolong is 'semi-fermented' and black tea is 'fermented'. Unfermented means that the fresh leaves are dried or steamed immediately after picking to prevent oxidization and the enzymes remain inactivated.

White tea is a speciality of Fujian province in China and is unique in that the fresh leaves undergo only two processes: withering and drying. The name 'white tea' comes from the delicate silvery white down or hairs that cover the leaves. Two main types of white tea are Yin Zhen, which means 'silver needles' and Pai Mu Tan, which means 'white peony'. For Yin Zhen the topmost bud is plucked early in the morning before the bud has opened and handled very carefully to protect the delicate white hairs. The buds are dried in the sun for two days then gently heat-dried and packed. Pai Mu Tan is processed in a similar way but from the secondary bud and proximate two leaves. Both teas have a light bouquet and delicate flavour. White tea has been cultivated and manufactured in China for at least 1,000 years. It is now also produced in Darjeeling, Sri Lanka and Assam.

Yellow tea is rare and only produced in China. The bud and first leaf are plucked and heated. The dampened leaves are wrapped in paper and allowed to dry slowly and mellow. This can take several days. Then they are heat dried. The leaves have a yellow, golden appearance, as does the liquor in the cup. Yellow tea has a light, mild taste.

Also unfermented is the better-known green tea. There are many types and the colour, appearance and fragrance of green teas vary considerably according to how they are processed. In China the freshly plucked leaves are dried (roasted) in heated copper basins or panning machines over a fire, more quickly than for yellow tea. They are then rolled either by hand or machine to give the leaf a particular appearance – some are twisted, some curved and some rolled. In Japan the process is a slightly different. The leaves are sweated in a steam tank until they become soft and pliable enough to roll and then are dried. The operation is repeated several times; after a final drying the leaves are sorted into various categories. Japan also produces a powdered green tea called *matcha*. It is this tea which is used in the *cha-no-yu* tea ceremony. After the leaves are dried with hot air and then sweated, they are chopped into tiny pieces, dried again and then ground into a fine powder.

Semi-fermented teas are called Oolong, which means 'black dragon' in Chinese. According to legend, the owner of a tea plantation was scared away from the tea leaves by the appearance of a black serpent. When he returned several days later the leaves had been oxidized by the sun and made a delicious tea. A more likely explanation for the name is that when the leaves are mixed with hot water they look like little black dragons.

Exactly when the process for oolong was discovered is unknown. According to one theory it was first invented in the Wuyi mountains of Fujian Province in the sixteenth century, where oolong teas are still renowned. However, since the mid-1880s Taiwan (formerly Formosa) has produced some of the world's finest oolongs.

Oolong teas can be made from young leaves or larger mature leaves which are semi-fermented; that is, the fermentation process is arrested early, producing a tea that combines the sweet scent of green tea with the delicate aroma of black. Oolong teas range from greenish rolled oolongs which have a light flowery flavour to dark brown-leafed oolongs which produce much earthier flavours, some with a hint of peach. These two distinct types are made by two quite different processes.

The Chinese method produces the lighter green oolongs. The leaf is first withered, then wrapped inside a large cloth and rolled in a special machine. The cloth is then opened and the leaf spread out to oxidize very briefly. The leaf is repeatedly wrapped, rolled and oxidized until approximately 15 to 30 per cent oxidization has taken place. The tea is then dried to remove all but two to three per cent of the remaining water. In Taiwan the freshly plucked leaf is withered, then shaken in bamboo baskets or in a bamboo tumbling machine. This lightly bruises parts of the leaf. The leaf is oxidized up to about 60 or 70 per cent and then dried.

Many oolong teas have lovely names, such as Shui Xian, which means 'water sprite', and Huang Jin Gui, meaning 'yellow golden flower'. The most famous and sought-after oolong is the fragrant Tie Guan Yin, named after Guanyin, the Iron Goddess of Mercy, which is made in both China and in Taiwan. It is often brewed *gongfu* style in tiny pottery teapots and sipped from thimble-sized cups.

Black tea is completely fermented. In the West it is called 'black tea' because the tea leaves turn a very dark colour whereas the Chinese and Japanese call it 'red tea' due to the reddish colour of the liquor. It was first produced in China during the Ming dynasty (1368–1644). During this time the fashion was for steeped tea using loose tea leaves which were just steamed and dried. Tea for trade, however, was still compressed into cakes, which travelled well and kept longer than loose tea, which quickly lost its aroma and flavour. Foreign trade was increasing with the West and tea was much in demand. A method was needed to produce tea that could retain its qualities during long journeys. Producers discovered that by fermenting the leaves in air (after first being withered, then bruised by rolling) until they turned a copper red colour and then halting the natural decomposition by baking, the leaves could be preserved.

There are two major types of black tea in China: plain and smoky. Plain black teas of China include Yunnan, Sichuan Imperial and Keemun. Smoky teas were first developed in Chongan County in the seventeenth century. It is said that the smoky flavour was discovered by accident when some soldiers camped in a tea factory filled with fresh leaves and processing was delayed. When the soldiers left the workers realized that it was too late to dry the tea leaves in the usual way if they were to get the tea to market in time. So they lit open fires of pine wood to speed up the drying process. Lapsang souchong is perhaps the best known of the smoky teas.

India is the world's leading producer of black tea and produces many fine varieties with varying tastes and flavours, such as the delicate teas of Darjeeling and the earthy strong teas of Assam. Sri Lanka (formerly Ceylon) also produces many fine black teas, most of which are used for blending, as do a number of African and South American countries. Africa ranks fourth in world tea production.

Puerh city in Yunnan, a province in the far southwest of China, gave its name to Puerh teas (sometimes referred to as compressed teas or more confusingly 'black tea'), which were first produced during the Tang dynasty (AD 618–906). Although never a production centre for tea, Puerh city was an important trading centre and it was from here that the merchants and traders set out with their cargo of teas along the *Chamadao* or *Chamagudao*, the ancient tea-horse road leading to Tibet, Burma and further afield.

Strictly speaking Puerh tea has to be made in Yunnan (although many other regions now produce similar teas) and the most famous place for production is Xishuangbanna. The tea trees, many of which are said to be between five hundred and a thousand years old, are located across six mountains. Puerh is a fermented tea made from what is known as the Big Leaf

Drying tea in China in the late 18th century.

('Da Ye'), a cultivar of *Camellia sinensis*. The tea trees, many of which are said to be between five hundred and a thousand years old, are located across six mountains. The leaves are plucked by climbing the trees, which can often be in inaccessible places. Early legends, thought to be inspired by Buddhist priests, tell of monkeys being used to gather the tea leaves from these trees. It is said the monkeys were trained to do this work, but other stories relate that when they were seen climbing the trees the Chinese would throw stones at them. The monkeys retaliated by breaking off tea branches and throwing them at their tormentors.[1]

There are two types of Puerh: naturally fermented (raw) and purposely fermented (cooked). The processing starts with picking; natural withering; hand firing in a hot wok to kill the enzymes in the leaf; hand rolling the leaf to squeeze out the moisture; and sun drying. The tea then goes through different processing stages depending on whether it is to be raw or cooked Puerh.

For raw Puerh the sun-dried loose tea may be pressed into cakes straight away, although usually they are left for a month or even a year before being weighed into correct portions and then compressed in metal moulds through which steam is passed. The steam softens the leaves and makes them pliable for compressing into cakes.

Puerh tea improves with age. The cakes can be matured for long periods, 50 years or more, and these antique vintage teas can be very expensive. For example, the famous Song Ping cakes (300 g) produced between 1910 and 1920 have an approximate value of £17,500.

During the 1970s demand for Puerh teas in China grew to such an extent that the technique for cooked Puerh was developed in order to speed up the aging process. The Menghai Tea Factory is credited as being one of the first factories

'Method of gathering Tea by means of Monkeys', 1820s, anonymous engraving.

to make 'cooked' Puerh in 1973; the Kunming Tea Factory was another.

To make 'cooked' Puerh the dried loose tea leaves are laid in cotton wrapping or sacks and sprayed with a controlled amount of water. The tea is then left to mature for up to 90 days in a warm and humid atmosphere before being compressed.

Puerh teas, both raw and cooked, are compressed into different shapes and sizes although some are left as loose leaves. When compressed they can be round, usually made with a hollow on the underside that is formed by the way the loose leaves are steamed and transferred into a linen bag. The end of the bag is twisted to prevent the leaves from falling out during compression. The twisted end pressing on to the leaves forms the hollow. Seven cakes are stacked together and then wrapped in bamboo leaves. Discs called 'bing' are similar to the round discs but do not have a hollow. 'Tuancha' are balls which are made in different sizes. 'Tuocha' are shaped a bit like a bird's nest. There are also mushroom or heart shapes and melon or pumpkin, a shape which symbolizes good wealth and fortune. Some are pressed into flat rectangular brick shapes. The presses may leave an intended imprint on the tea, such as an artistic design or simply the pattern of the cloth with which the tea was pressed. Many powdered tea bricks are moistened with rice water in pressing to assure that the tea powder sticks together. The pressed 'bricks' are then left to dry in storage.

The colour of Puerh tea in the cup ranges from greenish yellow with young teas through golden to russet, and ruby red for the older teas. The flavour also varies considerably, ranging from astringent and raw with a 'grassy' taste to an earthy rich taste with a hint of smokiness. The flavour becomes smoother and more mellow in the older teas.

It should be noted that Puerh is just one type of compressed tea. Green, oolong and black teas can also be made into bricks or cakes. This technique was developed very early on in the history of tea. The bricks or cakes of tea were much easier to transport long distances and the tea kept for longer. When needed a chunk of tea would be broken off the brick, roasted, then ground to a powder and brewed.

## Grading and Blending

At the end of processing tea leaves are graded and this is done differently in different countries. Grading does not refer to the quality of the tea but to the size and appearance of the tea leaf. There are four grades: leaf, broken leaf, fannings and dust. After the tea leaves have emerged from the dryers they are sifted with graduated mesh sizes. Leaf grades consist of

Various Puerh aged black teas.

the larger leaves that are left after sifting and are classified as Orange Pekoe and Pekoe. Pekoe comes from the Chinese word *pak-ho* or *pek-ho*, which means 'white hair', referring to the white down which covers the underside of some kinds of tea leaves or buds. There are several explanations for the word 'orange'. Some suggest that it is a remaining reference to the Netherlands House of Orange, a powerful entity in the early days of tea trading; others say it refers to the colour of the tea bud when dried.

Broken grades consist of smaller, broken leaves. These teas infuse faster and yield more flavour and fragrance.

Fannings are very small, broken leaves and dust are the smallest particles left after sifting. They are often used in tea bags as they infuse rapidly and make a strong and robust brew.

After grading, teas are either packed as 'speciality' teas (also referred to as 'single source' or 'garden' teas) or blended with other teas. Teas are blended because, like wines, the flavour and quality of tea can vary due to annual or seasonal

# Some Tea-tasting Terms

*Body*: with a strong liquor.

*Brassy*: with a bitter taste.

*Bright*: with a good pronounced colour, usually orange or coppery.

*Brisk*: refreshing, lively.

*Clean*: a pure, neutral aroma.

*Coarse*: with a harsh and vegetable flavour.

*Dull*: an infusion which lacks clearness.

*Earthy*: with an unpleasant taste (usually caused by storing tea in damp conditions).

*Flaky*: badly manufactured, producing flat or badly rolled leaves.

*Flowery*: high quality.

*Golden*: a term used to describe tea containing light tips.

*Light*: pale but with a good aroma and fresh flavour.

*Malty*: with a hint of malt taste.

*Plain*: lacking is character, without freshness or aroma.

*Raw*: with a bitter flavour.

*Rich*: well balanced and of high quality.

*Round*: full flavoured.

*Smooth*: with a pleasant, well-rounded taste.

*Sweaty*: with an undesirable sour flavour.

*Tip*: the outer leaf of the bud, which is covered in tiny hairs that give golden flecks to the processed leaf. Tippy teas contain a high proportion of tips.

*Tired*: old and badly packed or stored. Can also refer to a tea which comes from old, exhausted bushes.

*Woody*: tasting of hay or grass.

Twinings tea tasters at work.

fluctuations in climate and sometimes in the production process. By blending tea merchants can achieve a consistent character. They can also create blends to suit different tastes and to suit drinking at different times of the day.

Tea blending is a skilled art, taking many years to learn. Expert tasters sample hundreds of teas a day to develop a particular blend which may contain as many as 15 to 35 different teas. A blend can be a tea company's signature. Twinings, who have remained at the forefront of the tea industry for more than three hundred years, have developed a number of famous blends, including the aromatic Earl Grey. Another famous tea taster and blender extraordinaire was James Raleigh (1907–1999) of Taylors of Harrogate. He and his team developed the popular blend of Yorkshire Tea in the 1970s.

Some teas are scented or flavoured with flowers, fruits, aromatic oils of spices and herbs. Jasmine is the most popular scented tea in China. The flowers are plucked in the morning

Flower tea served in the Huxingting Tea Room in the old Chinese quarter of Shanghai, China.

and kept in a cool place until nightfall. When they start to open and release their fragrance they are piled next to the tea leaves, which absorb the scent. The leaves are spread out and re-piled and the process repeated sometimes as many as seven times a month for superior grades. The leaves are then refired to remove any moisture. Another method is to alternate the flowers and tea leaves in layers in wooden chests. Other scented teas include litchi, orchid and rose congou.

There are also flowering teas. Tea buds (usually white or green) are hand-sewn together with fresh flowers such as jasmine or amaranth into tea balls or blossoms. When infused in hot water the 'blossom' unfurls almost magically into a floral display, and for this reason the tea is usually made in a transparent teapot for greater effect. These teas have been developed in the tea gardens of Yunnan.

These teas should not be confused with the amazing number and varieties of herbal teas (often called tisanes). They are not real teas and contain no product of the tea plant but are called 'tea' because they are made in a similar fashion by infusing leaves, either dried or fresh, or sometimes the flowers or roots of plants. The word tisane originates from the classical Greek *ptisane* meaning crushed barley. This passed via Latin (*ptisana)* into thirteenth-century French as *tisaine*.

These herbal infusions are often made for medicinal purposes, for alleviating or curing specific ailments or for refreshment. Flavour and health benefits determine the choice of plant. Most do not contain caffeine and have more delicate and milder flavours than true tea. Popular herbal teas include chamomile, ginger, peppermint, rose-hip and ginseng.

# 2
# China

There is very little accurate historical information about the beginning of tea-drinking in China. It is probable that by the first century BC people in Sichuan were infusing tea leaves in hot water. The first recognizable definition of tea, under the name of *kia*, or *k'u t'u*, with the additional information that it was a beverage 'made from the leaves by boiling', is in a Chinese dictionary, *Erh Ya*, annotated in about AD 350 by a Chinese scholar, Kuo P'o.[1]

A description of how to infuse tea leaves from pressed tea is found in an extract from the *Kuang Ya*, a dictionary by Chang i of the later Wei dynasty (AD 386–534):

> the leaves were plucked and made into cakes in the district between the provinces of Hupeh and Szechwan; the cakes were roasted until reddish in colour, pounded into tiny pieces, and placed in a chinaware pot. Boiling water was then poured over them, after which onion, ginger, and orange were added.[2]

Salt was also often added. At this time tea was a bitter medicinal drink used as a remedy for various ailments including stomach problems, lethargy and even bad eyesight.

By the end of the fifth century tea was being exported or traded with Turkish and Mongolian merchants, usually in the form of brick tea.

During the Tang Dynasty (618–907) China reached unparalleled prosperity. It was a glorious period and trade flourished. A better-quality tea emerged and it began to be drunk as a refreshing and stimulating beverage by members of the upper class, scholars and priests.

The new vogue of tea-drinking was not restricted to the Chinese, as Uyghur visitors to the capital of Chang'an (Xian) were enthusiastic tea-buyers. By the late eighth century tea was being exported to faraway places: to Japan; along the ancient tea-horse caravan road to Tibet and Burma; and along the Silk Road to Central Asia. In fact tea had become such big business that tea merchants commissioned Lu Yü, a poet and scholar, to write the first treatise on the subject. Called *Ch'a Ching* (The Classic of Tea), Lu Yü's book played a very important and everlasting role in the development of tea culture.

The exact date of Lu Yü's birth is not known, nor is his parentage, and there are varying accounts of his life. Most accounts agree that a Buddhist monk, Zhi Ji, found him abandoned as an infant near a lake and later in life raised him and taught him writing, poetry, chanting sutras and how to brew tea. Later Lu Yü travelled widely and along the way learned much about the cultivation of tea and the processing of tea leaves. Lu Yü went into seclusion some time between AD 760 and 762 and during this period he wrote his masterpiece, *Ch'a Ching*.

*Ch'a Ching* came out in AD 780 and was the earliest book about tea. It consisted of three slim volumes and was divided into ten parts. Lu Yü's writing is poetic but his book contains practical and detailed information about how tea should be made, what tools should be used, what kind of water is best, how to drink tea and so on, creating a sense of order and ritual in harmony with the Taoist spirit of the times. In the final section he advises tea enthusiasts to copy out all the sections of his book on silk scrolls and to hang them up for quick and ready reference at all times.

He describes tea as follows:

> Tea has a myriad of shapes. If I may speak vulgarly and rashly, tea may shrink and crinkle like a Mongol's boots. Or it may look like the dewlap of a wild ox, some sharp, some curling as the eaves of a house. It can look like a mushroom in whirling flight just as clouds do when they float out from behind a mountain's peak. Its leaves can swell and leap as if they were being lightly tossed on wind-disturbed water . . .

On the question of what water to use, he had the following advice:

> Tea made from mountain streams is best, river water is all right, but well-water tea is quite inferior . . . Water from the slow-flowing streams, the stone-lined pools or milk-pure springs is the best of mountain water. Never take tea made from water that falls in cascades, gushes from springs, rushes in a torrent or that eddies and surges as if nature were rinsing its mouth . . . Of the many other streams that flow through mountain and valley, there are those that are clear and pure but which sink into the ground and are absorbed before finding an outlet. From the hot season to the time of frost, the dragon may be sequestered and noxious poisons will accumulate within them. One taste of the water will tell you if it is all right.

> If the evil genius of a stream makes the water bubble like
> a fresh spring, pour it out.

And he instructs on making tea:

> When the water is boiling, it must look like fishes' eyes
> and give off but the hint of a sound. When at the edges
> it chatters like a bubbling spring and looks like pearls in-
> numerable strung together, it has reached the second stage.
> When it leaps like breakers majestic and resounds like a
> swelling wave, it is at its peak. Any more and the water will
> be boiled out and should not be used.[3]

During the Song dynasty (AD 960–1279), a period of
romanticism and elegant taste, the rustic brick tea fell out
of grace. Tea became more delicately flavoured and connoisseurs ground tea leaves to a fine powder, added boiling
water and whisked it to a froth. The tea was drunk alone
and enjoyed for its own flavour and aroma although occasionally it was scented with dried flowers such as jasmine
and roses.

Monks and priests continued to drink tea to help them
stay alert during meditation. It became an alternative to wine
for poets and writers who drank it for inspiration. One of
them was Tu Hsiao-Shan:

> One winter night
> A friend dropped in.
> We drank not wine but tea.
> The kettle hissed,
> The charcoal glowed,
> A bright moon shone outside.
> The moon itself

Was nothing special –
But, ah, the plum-tree blossom!⁴

Poets also began to give lyrical names to teas such as 'sparrow's tongues' and 'gray eyebrows'.

Emperor Huei Tsung (1101–1124) was a great tea connoisseur who was more dedicated to art and science than to politics. He wrote a dissertation on the twenty kinds of tea and proclaimed that white tea was the rarest and of the highest quality. At his court tea-drinking became a ritual of elegance and refinement. However, tea-drinking was not confined to the court or the educated classes. Tea-houses began to spring up in the big cities and tea-drinking spread to the middle and working classes through the Zen Buddhists, many of whom belonged to the lower classes. Tea-drinking played a role in Zen religious ceremonies and many of the rituals and customs were adopted by the Japanese in their own tea ceremony. Tea also became a homely beverage, drunk daily and served to guests.

Tea cultivation spread to other parts of China. But with the Mongol conquest of China in 1280 tea-drinking declined. Two famous travellers to China at this time, Marco Polo and William of Rubruk, did not mention tea in their journals.

Tea enjoyed a revival under the Ming Dynasty (1368–1644). The practice of steeping loose tea leaves in boiling water became common. Fermented black tea was developed at this time and tea-ware developed as an art form. Teapots were made in various shapes and today's round teapot is based on one of the Ming designs. The Yixing teapot became popular. These teapots, which were usually small, were ideal for bringing out all the aroma and flavour of the tea leaves. To complement the size of the small teapots the tea was sipped from tiny handleless cups.

Tea began to be traded with the West. Foreign traders, travellers, ambassadors and missionaries began to visit China, sample the tea and eventually take it home with them.

The tradition of public tea-houses in China began as early as the Tang dynasty (618–906). They were places for relaxation and leisure. Tea-houses flourished through the centuries and became places of artistic culture, where mainly the wealthy classes came to drink tea, socialize and perhaps discuss politics. Calligraphy and paintings often decorated the walls. Tea-houses became open to everyone, including labourers and craftsmen, who came to relax after a hard day's work. Tea-houses in Hangzhou were noted for their scholarly atmosphere while those of Chengdu, the capital of Sichuan, were well known for their storytelling, ballad singing and *kuaiban* (rhythmic verses accompanied by bamboo clappers).[5]

The tea-house tradition continued, varying in style in different parts of China, reflecting differences in climate, topography and culture.

Yixing teapots are made from *zisha*, a purple-sand clay found only in the region of the town of Yixing in Jiangsu province, China. What makes a Yixing teapot special is that the inside is never glazed and, because of its porous nature, it absorbs the flavour of the tea brewed in it. Over a period of time, the pot literally becomes infused with the tea flavour.

Yixing teapots for sale in Yu Yuan Bazaar, Old City, Shanghai, China.

Fu Baoshi (1904–65), *Playing Weiqi at the Water Pavilion*, mid-20th century, hanging scroll, ink and colour on paper. Tea has been served in the pavilion.

Crowds of people in a tea-house inside the Manjushiri Monastery in Chengdu, China.

Up until the 1940s tea-houses were at the centre of Sichuanese social life. Some were frequented by members of Sichuan's secret societies, who used the arrangement of their teacups as an elaborate secret code. Some tea-houses specialized in storytelling or theatrical performances, in some chess was played and others were notorious as rendezvous for prostitutes and their clients.

After the Communists came to power in 1949 most people were too busy working and building the future of the country to gather in tea-houses and their business declined. During the Cultural Revolution they were seen as 'subversive' and most closed down altogether. Since the late 1970s there has been a revival. A more relaxed attitude and a desire for some of the old traditions to return have ensured that tea-houses are thriving once again in China although many are now different from the past, more modern and less authentic.

Chung Feng De Yi Lou tea-house in Yu Yuan Bazaar, Shanghai, China.

The Green Tea House in Beijing, China.

Chinese food expert Fuchsia Dunlop describes the manner of serving tea at a Sichuan tea-house:

> The Sichuanese rarely use teapots, but brew their loose tea leaves in individual china bowls with lids and saucers (this is known as 'lid-bowl tea' – *gai wan cha*). The saucer catches spills and protects the drinker from the hotness of the cup; the bowl is the drinking vessel; and the lid is used to keep the tea hot and, with a gentle sweeping motion, to help the water circulate as the leaves infuse. Sichuanese tea-drinkers also use the lid as a filter, fanning away any floating tea-leaves as they raise the bowl to their lips. In teahouses, each new guest is given a tea-bowl with a layer of dry tea-leaves in the bottom. The hot water is added at the table, and the tea-bowl covered as the liquid infuses. The first brewing can have a bitter taste (some connoisseurs even throw it away): the second brewing is thought to be the best. The water is topped up at regular intervals by the tea attendants with their copper kettles, some with

the famous yard-long spouts which are handled with flamboyance and amazing dexterity. The same cup of tea can last as long as you want it to, although the flavour of the leaves obviously weakens with each refilling.[6]

Tea-house culture in the south, notably in Canton and Hong Kong, developed in a different way. The custom of *yum cha*, a term in Cantonese which means 'drink tea', became popular. Tea was served in tiny porcelain cups with delectable, hot bite-sized savoury snacks called dim sum (loosely translating as 'heart warmers'). Men would go early in the morning for *yum cha* and, as the saying goes, over 'a pot of tea and two dimsum', would discuss business, perhaps until lunch time.[7] With the rise of Canton and Hong Kong as bustling trading ports in the nineteenth century, tea-houses became emporium-type restaurants, many of which served dim sum from trolleys which were wheeled around for customers to choose from. Today dim sum are more likely to be ordered from a menu.

Business discussions over a cup of tea in a tea-house are no doubt very important but tea also plays a part in the serious business of marriage. The old custom of sending a present of tea to the girl's family is still observed in China. When the tea is accepted it means she is engaged. The tea is symbolic because the tea plant cannot be grafted but must be planted by seedling. This characteristic of the tea plant suggests loyalty, oneness and abidingness – the best symbols of a lasting engagement.

Another custom is for the bride to offer to her mother-in-law, with both hands, a cup of tea sweetened with a couple of crystallized lotus seeds and honey as a gesture of affection and obedience and an expression of the wish to bear her grandsons, implied by the symbolic lotus seeds. The mother-in-law will then sip the tea, signifying that the affection will be returned in kind, often in the form of sparkling jewellery.[8]

## China's Teas

Techniques for tea cultivation until the nineteenth century remained much the same as they had been from very early days. Nowadays much of the manufacture of tea has been mechanized, although some skilled hand-production is still carried on.

Today tea is cultivated in almost every province of China except for cold regions such as Mongolia and Tibet. Many of China's tea gardens are found in small patches high in the mountains. Village farmers grow a majority of the tea. The plucked leaves are taken to the village tea factory or local cooperative factory for processing. Taste preferences for different types of tea vary from region to region and each tea-producing region is famous for unique teas which have been perfected over the generations.

China produces many celebrated and distinctive teas: the rare white and yellow teas, delicate green teas such as chun mee and gunpowder, fragrant oolong such as Shui Xian (water sprite), and black teas such as keemun and the smoky Lapsang Souchong and Puerh teas.

One of the most famous green teas is Long Jing (Dragon Well tea), from an area in Hangzhou, Zhejiang Province called Dragon Well, which is famed for its scenic landscape and historic and cultural heritage. The name Dragon Well derives from a local spring, which according to legend is the lair of a dragon. Emperor Qianlong (r. 1735–96) was staying near today's Dragon Well during one of his inspection tours and drank tea there. He was so delighted with it that he named it

Preparing Long Jing tea.

Dragon Well tea and granted it the status of *Gong Cha* or Imperial Tea. The Emperor it seems was also responsible for the distinctive shape of the prepared tea leaves. While out strolling he picked some tea leaves and liked their appearance so much he pressed them between the pages of a book. The flattened leaves were later used to make some tea, which had a very pleasing taste. In memory of the Emperor's visit the tea farmers still use a laborious drying process to make the tea leaves flat.

Eighteen royal tea trees still stand in Dragon Well. Drinking Dragon Well tea made from the first spring picking and made with water from the well, is said to be the ultimate tea drinker's experience. It is considered by connoisseurs to be the finest of Chinese teas and is traditionally served to emperors, kings, queens and presidents. When the late Premier Chou En Lai invited President Nixon to Hangzhou during his first trip to China in the spring of 1972 they not only signed the Shanghai Communiqué, which normalized relations between China and the US, but also drank Dragon Well tea together. Dragon Well tea was also given as a present to Queen Elizabeth II of Great Britain on her first state visit to China in 1986.

Dragon Well is praised for its 'four uniques' or 'four wonders': its emerald or jade green colour; aromatic flavour; sweet and mellow taste; and beautiful shape or appearance. This is achieved by the method of growing and processing. The long, thin tea leaves are grown in the shade and the best quality leaves are picked before the spring rain falls. They are then hand-wrapped and dried so that the bright green colour and shape are retained.

Dragon Well tea is used as a flavouring in a shrimp dish. The green tea imparts a fresh and cool flavour. Other teas are also used in cooking. Tea-smoked duck is one of the most famous delicacies of Sichuan Province. Traditionally the duck is smoked over a mixture of jasmine tea, cypress or pine twigs and sawdust, which imparts a distinctive smoky and aromatic flavour to the duck. Tea eggs, sometimes called marbled eggs, are another speciality. They are a typical Chinese savoury snack commonly sold by street vendors in most Chinese communities throughout the world.

# 3

# Japan, Korea and Taiwan

Tea-drinking and the rituals connected with it play a very important part in the Japanese way of life. The tea ceremony, *cha-no-yu*, which means 'hot-water-tea' and is also called *chado*, 'The Way of Tea', was originally a Buddhist ritual. Monks drank powdered tea from a communal bowl before an image of Bodhidharma. In the late fourteenth century a Zen priest called Shuko combined the rituals of preparing and drinking of tea with a spiritual sense of humility and tranquillity, thus creating the tea ceremony. He became the first great tea master and it was he who prepared an austere code of rules.

In the sixteenth century Zen tea master Sen Rikyu (1522–1591) amended the ceremony to the form it has today. The ritual is less elaborate and focuses on harmony, respect, purity and serenity. When asked by one of his disciples what the most important things were in following the 'Way of Tea', he proposed the observance of seven rules:

> Make a delicious bowl of tea:
> Lay out the wood charcoal to heat the water.
> Arrange the flowers as they are in the fields.
> In summer, evoke coolness; in winter, warmth.
> Anticipate the time for everything.

Be prepared for rain.

Show the greatest attention to each of your guests.

The tea ceremony influenced all Japan's fine arts, including garden design, flower arrangement, architecture, calligraphy, painting, lacquer and ceramic arts. It has developed into an elaborate social custom.

The ceremony takes place in a special pavilion (*chashitsu*), which is reached via a winding garden path symbolic of a mountain path, and begins with *cha kaiseki*. This is the meal served at the beginning of a full tea ceremony, since it is not thought good to drink strong powdered tea on an empty stomach. Hot dishes are served in various courses. First there is a tray bearing a bowl of rice, miso soup, and a dish of vinegared fish or vegetables, or *sashimi*. Saké is poured by the host, then *nimono* (simmered food) is served, followed by *yakimono* (grilled food). A light broth or soup called *suimono* is then served 'to wash the chopsticks'. Rare delicacies follow, representing the bounty of both land and sea. Finally a pickle called *ko no mono* is served with *yuto* (hot washings of the rice pot, served in a lacquerware container shaped like a teapot without a handle).

Just before the green tea is served, a sweet confection called *wagashi* is eaten to offset the tea's bitterness. These are the Japanese equivalent of confectionery, cakes, cookies and candy. There are many different types. *Wagashi* are often very beautiful and may reflect the various faces of nature in Japan's four seasons.[1]

After *cha kaiseki* the guests retire to the garden. This gives the host time to tidy up after the meal and prepare for the main part of the ceremony *(cha-no-yu)*. When all is ready the guests are invited to re-enter the tearoom for the drinking of *matcha*, powdered green tea. The etiquette is quite

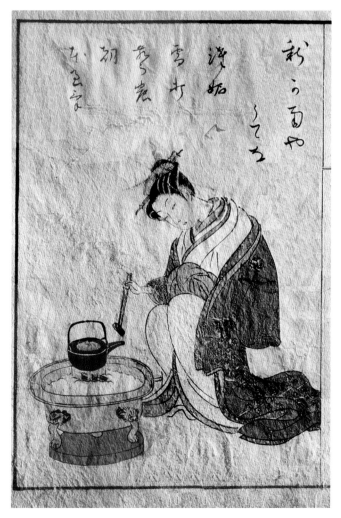

A woodblock print depicting a Japanese lady preparing water for tea.

The principal guest is complimenting the host on the tea after the first sip in a Japanese tea ceremony in the 1930s.

complicated and elaborate; tea-making utensils and tea bowls as well as the decorations in the tea room are carefully chosen and coordinated in keeping with *wabi* aesthetics (*wabi* meaning understated beauty). First a very rich thick paste-like mixture called *koicha* is made by kneading *matcha*. It is prepared for each guest in succession, the same bowl being cleaned and reused. The tea is bitter and strong and is drunk in its entirety. It is considered mandatory to make some appreciative comment on the beauty of the setting, the utensils and so on. The tea ceremony concludes with the drinking of *usucha*, a foamy infusion which is made using less *matcha* and more water. The *matcha*, which is kept in a lacquered tea box or caddy called a *chaire*, is scooped into the tea bowl (*chawan*) by a special teaspoon or scoop called a *chasaku*. Hot water is added and then whisked vigorously with a bamboo whisk (*chasen*) to produce a pale green liquid with a light surface froth.

What is the background history to this elaborate tea ceremony? The knowledge of tea was probably brought to Japan from China in the late sixth century at the same time as Buddhism. During the Tang dynasty many Japanese priests pursued their studies of Buddhism in China and brought back various customs, including the use of brick tea (called *dancha* in Japan), which was the favoured drink of China at that time.

In AD 729 Emperor Shomu invited 100 Buddhist monks to his palace at Nara to read from Buddhist scriptures for four days. He served them a rare and costly beverage: *hiki-cha* or powdered tea, which had been brought to him by emissaries at the Tang court. The tea, which was a thick liquid and high in caffeine, was made by whisking powdered green tea with boiling water. It enabled the monks to stay alert during the long hours of reading the scriptures. And, not long after Lu Yü had written *Ch'a Ching* during the Tang dynasty in China, a Japanese monk called Saicho (also known by his later name of Dengyo Daishi), who had been studying in China, brought back some seeds for tea plants and planted them in the temple grounds at Yeisan.

In AD 815 tea was served to the Emperor Saga. He was so impressed that he ordered tea to be planted in five provinces and declared tea the beverage of the court. However, at that time, as in China, it was considered more as a health drink or medicine than a beverage.

The 'Drink of Ceremony', as it was known in Japan, was prepared as Lu Yü had advised in his book. Tea was sipped during poetry readings and given all the respect it commanded in China. It was this ceremony which was to develop much later into the complex ritual of the Japanese tea ceremony. However, after the death of Emperor Saga tea drinking declined. This was because of civil strife in Japan as well as political upheavals in China. For about three hundred years tea was more or less forgotten, except in Buddhist temples where it remained part of religious ritual and helped keep the monks awake during the long hours of meditation.

On the return of peace and stability, tea cultivation resumed. Trade links with the Chinese were also thriving. A priest known as Eisai, who had been studying at the great Zen monasteries in China, returned to Japan with new seeds and reintroduced tea cultivation. In AD 1191 he wrote the first tea book in Japan, *Kitcha-Yojoki* ('The Book of Tea Sanitation'). It was really a health book and the health benefits of tea were well appreciated when he was called to the bedside of a sick samurai. The samurai was probably only suffering from the after-effects of too much good food and alcohol but Yeisei administered some green tea. The samurai recovered and tea was acclaimed as a miracle beverage.

During the thirteenth century the custom of drinking *matcha* first reached the temples and the upper level of samurai society. It then spread to the common people, who began to drink tea as an enjoyable beverage rather than as a health drink or medicine.

By the fourteenth and fifteenth centuries parties based on a tea-drinking game called *tôcha* were common. *Tôcha* was a guessing game where players would be served several varieties of tea from different districts and a prize was awarded to the person who correctly identified the most varieties. A fourteenth-century document entitled 'Conventions of Tea Drinking' (*Kissa ôrai*) described the *tôcha* party. It started with three rounds of saké. This was followed by a dish of noodles and a cup of tea and then a main course consisting of various delicacies, finishing off with a dessert of fruits. The guests then retired to the garden for a while before gathering together for the game, which was held in a special room where the various teas were served with sweets. After the game 'the tea utensils were put away and rounds of saké drinking ensued with entertainments of song, music and dance'.[2]

Tea-drinking reached a very high level in Japan under the distinguished patronage of the 8th Shogun, Yoshimasa (1435–1490). Tea became so popular that it was sold by vendors outside temples, eventually leading to the first tea rooms of Japan. In Kyoto people can visit Yoshimasa's Ginkaku-ji, or Silver Pavilion, which housed the first tea room. It was here that Yoshimasa practised the rites of the *cha-no-yu*, or tea ceremony, during his later years in retirement.

It was not until the late sixteenth century that loose leaf tea was imported from China and in Japan was known as *sencha*. *Sencha* became Japan's most popular everyday tea because it was cheaper and easier to make than the powdered *matcha* tea. *Sencha* is a green tea and various qualities are manufactured, the best being served to guests and for special occasions when the tea is to be savoured rather than just used to quench thirst. The leaves are processed by first steaming then fluffing in hot air, then dried and rolled into fine needles. The tea is brewed at 80°C (176°F) and steeped for one minute.

*Bancha*, the lowest grade of *sencha*, is the everyday tea of Japan. It is drunk at breakfast as a refreshing start to the day. It is a coarse green tea full of twigs and is made from older leaves. To improve the flavour it is sometimes roasted, in which case it is called *hojicha*. When brewed (with boiling water), *hojicha* has a slightly smoky flavour. This tea is drunk throughout the day, even at bedtime, since it contains less caffeine than other teas.

*Genmaicha* is another kind of *bancha*. Grains of rice (*genmai*) are roasted until they pop and mixed with *bancha*. The resulting tea, made with boiling water, has an aromatic, nutty flavour.

*Gyokuro*, which means 'drops of dew', is the finest and most expensive of Japanese teas. It is made from the very young buds of old tea bushes that are protected from the sun by straw matting for three weeks before plucking in order to produce more chlorophyll and less tannin. Only the best leaves are used. After steaming the leaves are basket-fired and hand-rolled to produce beautifully shaped flat and pointed needles of an emerald colour. The tea, which is brewed at a low temperature in a small teapot called *kyusu*, has a smooth taste and subtle perfume. It is served in small quantities and savoured in the mouth before swallowing.

*Tencha* is of the same class as *gyokuro* in that the leaves are also shaded from sunlight before harvesting but is different in that the leaves are not rolled but are finely chopped. It is this tea which is ground into a fine powder called *matcha*, the tea used in the tea ceremony. Only ground *tencha* qualifies as *matcha*. *Matcha uji* means 'froth of liquid jade'. Other green teas which are powdered are known as *konacha* ('powder tea').

Today many kinds of leaf tea are drunk in Japan. Most are green teas but some black teas imported from Ceylon and India are popular and are on the menus of leading hotels and restaurants. Black tea is always drunk from Western-style teacups, whereas green tea is always drunk in Japanese-style cups or, if the tea is powdered, from tea bowls.

Japanese people like to go to tea-houses called *kissaten* and often entertain guests there rather than at home. If the tea being served is black it might be accompanied by *kasutera*, a sweet sponge cake introduced to Japan in the sixteenth century by the Portuguese. If the tea is *matcha, wagashi* might be served with it.

The Japanese produce high-quality green tea but exports have dwindled recently due to the high costs of land and

Tea bushes being shaded so that the leaves develop a good flavour in Nishio, Japan.

*Camellia sinensis* plant in Nishio, Japan.

labour. Green teas are produced in large gardens in the regions of Shizuoka, Mie, Kagoshima, Kyoto, Nara and Saitama. The most exclusive green teas in Japan are produced in Uji, on the plains where the soil is particularly good. The most prized Uji tea is *gyokuro*. The best teas come from plants grown from cuttings of Eisai's tea bushes at the Reisen-ji Temple garden, which were planted in the twelfth century.

Japanese teas are sometimes used as a flavouring in cooking. A tea jelly called *kanten* is popular, as is green tea ice cream made with *matcha*. *O-chazuke* is a rice dish flavoured with tea.

# Korea

Like its neighbours, Korea has a rich tea-drinking culture. Green tea (*nok ch'a*) was introduced from Tang China during the reign of Queen Sŏndŏk (AD 632–647) although tea drinking might have been known much earlier. Tea was initially prized for its medicinal properties and was also reserved for special occasions. King Munmu, who ruled from 661 to 681, ordered tea to be used during ceremonial offerings.

Tea-drinking in Korea is linked with the *Panyaro Seon* (Zen) of tea and is viewed as a spiritual, religious activity leading to higher levels of inner awakening, if not total enlightenment. Buddhist monks commonly drank tea as an aid to meditation and offered tea to the Buddha three times daily. Temples also served tea to visitors. Due to such demand for tea, villages arose near to temples that cultivated tea and became known as *tach'on*, or 'tea villages'.

It was not until the reign of the 42nd Silla monarch, King Heungdeok (826–836), that a royal envoy Kim Taeryom

Whisked green tea, Korea.

returned from a mission in Tang dynasty China and brought seeds of the tea plant. The king ordered the seeds to be planted on the warm slopes of Mount Chiri, which is still the centre of tea cultivation in Korea.

The ceremonies related to drinking tea at the royal court and elsewhere developed into the custom known as the tea ceremony (*tado*). Specialized implements for this ceremony were developed, such as a brazier for boiling water, bowls for water and tea, spoons and pots. Types and qualities of tea were also developed, as was a grading system for the taste of water. As in Japan, tea ceremony etiquette is very important in Korea but the harmony of water and tea is even more central to the ritual. Üisun (1786–1866), the famous monk and tea-master, wrote: 'In brewing, delicacy, in storing, aridity, in steeping, purity. Delicacy, aridity, and purity are essential to the tea ceremony.'[3]

Other 'teas' popular with Koreans are not true teas. They are made from fruits such as quince, citron and jujubes or from other ingredients such as ginseng, ginger and cinnamon. All are drunk for their medicinal properties. *Pori ch'a*, barley 'tea', made with roasted barley and boiling water and served hot or cold, is the standard beverage drunk with a meal.

## Taiwan (Formosa)

The first Europeans to visit Taiwan were Portuguese sailors in the sixteenth century. They were so impressed by its beauty that they called it Isla Formosa, meaning 'Beautiful Island', and it was called Formosa until the Chinese renamed the island Taiwan. The island has ideal conditions for growing tea due to its geographical position, the mountainous terrain and a temperature that never drops below 12 °C (55 °F).

The first tea seedlings were brought by immigrants from China's Fujian province who came across the Taiwan Straits in the mid-1850s and settled in Taiwan. They not only brought with them tea seedlings and tea-growing and processing skills but their tea culture as well. However, large-scale tea production did not start until about 1866, when English investors imported tea seedlings from China. Taiwan produces green and black teas but is best known for its oolong teas.

One of the most famous and rarest oolong teas from Taiwan is 'Oriental Beauty', (the name, it is said, was bestowed upon it by Queen Elizabeth II when she was presented a sample by a British tea merchant). The tea is also sometimes known as Champagne Formosa and it is highly appreciated by connoisseurs for its deep reddish gold liquor and fruity, rich and smooth taste. Other famous oolongs include Oolong Imperial, Grand Oolong Fancy, Tung Ting and a lightly fermented tea called pouchong.

Tea was an important export commodity until the 1980s but today most of the tea is bought and consumed by the tea-loving Taiwanese. Many enjoy their tea at specially designed tea houses that provide a peaceful atmosphere with no outside windows and are constructed around a central courtyard that usually has a fish pond. Tea houses are also cultural establishments which often display calligraphy and paintings and offer concerts of traditional music.

The Taiwanese love of tea has also resulted in a new trend, called bubble tea, which has since caught on in other parts of the world, including the Philippines and North America, especially where there is a large Chinese population. The drink originally started as a treat in the late 1980s for thirsty children who after lessons delighted in buying refreshing tea at tea-stands outside school. One innovative concession holder, to the joy of her clientele, started to add different fruit flavourings

Creamy bubble green tea.

to her milky tea, which she then shook vigorously to mix everything together. Bubbles formed on top.

The children loved the new dimension to the sweet, cool taste of their tea and other concession holders followed suit. Someone then had the idea of adding tapioca pearls to the tea. These pearls sank to the bottom of the cup, thus creating bubbles on the bottom and bubbles on top. Bubble tea is usually served in see-through plastic cups or containers with an extra wide straw to suck up the pearls which have a soft and chewy consistency. And, for even more fun, the children sometimes like to blow the balls out from the straw to shoot at targets or even each other! Bubble tea has acquired many names, some of them wacky, such as boba, QQ (which means chewy in Chinese), and in the West 'booboo'.

# 4
# Caravans and
# Mediterranean Shores

During the Tang Empire (618–906) in China a thriving inter-Asian trade developed and tea trading became big business. Two main overland trade routes went from China. The ancient *Chamadao* ('Tea-Horse Road') linked China's south-west provinces of Yunnan and Sichuan with Tibet, Burma and beyond. To the north the Silk Road linked China with Central Asia, the Middle East and the Mediterranean. Another trading route, the Siberian Route, which opened up much later, linked China with Russia via Siberia and became known as the Tea Road.

The idea of trading caravans evokes a romantic image. In reality, these journeys were fraught with dangers and hardships. The caravans travelled long distances, often over barren deserts, high mountain passes and along jungle trails. Traders and travellers were in constant danger of being attacked or robbed by brigands so they would travel for safety in a 'caravan'.

Tea was usually carried in brick form. The tea kept better and it made for easier transportation. The bricks could be sewn into yak skins to withstand knocks and bad weather. The universality of brick tea in Tibet and surrounding areas led to its use as a form of currency for bartering. Tea bricks were also the preferred form of currency over metallic coins for the nomads of Mongolia and Siberia.

## *Chamadao* ('Tea-Horse Road')

Tea and horses were the most important commodities traded along this ancient and rugged road, which was also sometimes called the South Silk Road. As with the better known Silk Road to the north, this route was never a single path but a patchwork of established trails crisscrossing the mountains and jungles. Two main routes went to Nepal and India via Lhasa, the capital of Tibet. One began at the original site of the famous Puerh tea production in Yunnan; the other at Ya'an in Sichuan. Other routes linked China with Burma, leading to India, Laos and Vietnam, and one route went north to Beijing. During the Tang and Song dynasties trade flourished along this road but by the early twentieth century it had generally been abandoned as a trading route.

It is said that tea was first introduced to Tibet in the year AD 641 when the Chinese Princess Wen Cheng married the Tibetan King Songstan Gambo. Tibetans welcomed tea, which quickly became a local staple.

Tea cannot be grown in Tibet because of the rugged climate and cold winters so merchants made the long arduous trek to Yunnan to obtain supplies. Meanwhile the Chinese lacked strong war horses needed for fighting hostile neighbours to the north and west, which Tibet could supply.

Instead of adopting the Chinese way of tea-drinking Tibetans found other ways of preparing it which not only provided warmth but also extra nutrition. Vegetables do not grow well in the harsh climate and were rarely eaten in Tibet. Tea counter-balanced a heavy reliance on meat and dairy

Men laden with tea bricks for Tibet.

products and also helped digestion. They devised a rich brew resulting in what could be called a 'soup'.

The tea, called *bo-jha* or *po cha*, referred to in the west as 'butter tea', can be made in a number of ways. It is usually made from brick tea. Chunks of tea are broken off the brick, which are first toasted over a fire to destroy any infestation by moulds or insects. The tea is boiled in water for five to ten

Rinjing Dorje's sketch
of a Tibetan woman
making tea in a churn.

minutes until dark and strong, then strained into a wooden
or bamboo tea churn. Yak milk, yak butter and salt are added
and the mixture churned vigorously with a stick. When the
tea is ready to drink it is poured into a plain earthenware
teapot and then served in wooden tea bowls.

Rinjing Dorje, a Tibetan who now lives in the USA, wrote
the first book in English to describe Tibetan foods and their
relation to Tibetan culture. He explains how it is drunk:

After [tea] is served, we let it sit for a while before drinking
it. At least three to five cups of tea are considered necessary for everyone in the morning. And we always say a
prayer of offering to the holy ones before drinking. Then
we pick up the cup and carefully blow all the butter that

is floating on the top of the tea to one side. If you save the butter in this way, it is good when you finish your tea to put some *tsampa* [roasted flour, usually barley] in the cup and mix this with it.[1]

Ladakh, a region of northern India bordering on Tibet and sometimes called 'Little Tibet' as it has been strongly influenced by Tibetan culture, makes butter tea in a similar way.

The Burmese people also devised their own way of preparing tea, as a dish, using pickled tea leaves called *lephet*. Tender tea leaves are steamed and then pressed tightly into clay vessels or large bamboo stems. These containers are

Butter tea churns in a Tibetan kitchen.

A modern Burmese lacquered *lephet* tray containing pickled tea leaves (*lephet*) in the centre compartment, surrounded by the other traditional accompaniments to be eaten with it.

stored in the ground, preferably close to a river bed to ensure an even temperature.

*Lephet* is served with a variety of garnishes and these are traditionally served in a special lacquer box made up of different compartments, each being filled with *lephet*, dried shrimps, fried slices of garlic, toasted sesame seeds, fried crisp broad beans (*pegyi*), roasted peanuts, dried peas fried crisply (*pelon*) and salt. Some of these boxes were made for court use and were very elaborate. *Lephet* is a stimulant and is often eaten after a rich meal to clear the palate. It is usually accompanied by a cup of tea. It is eaten by taking a pinch with the tips of three fingers, together with two or three items of the garnishes. In between bites the fingers are wiped and sips of tea are taken. Finger bowls are provided at the end.

The Burmese also drink green tea at teashops and a 'sweet tea', sold at stalls which were originally run by Indian immigrants, has also become popular. It is made with milk and sugar and is very much like the *chai* of India. The tea is boiled and then sweetened with condensed milk, resulting in a pinkish brown beverage which is thick and strong. Here, instead of asking for green or black tea, one asks for 'mildly sweet', 'mildly sweet and strong', 'sweet and rich,' or 'Kyaukpadaung' (very sweet and thick).[2]

In Vietnam today you are more likely to see people drinking coffee but tea-drinking has a long history and green tea is still part of the culture, with its own social and cultural ceremonies. King Tu Duc, who reigned during the Nguyen dynasty (1848–1883) in the ancient capital of Hue on the central coast, was renowned for drinking a special lotus-flavoured tea. In the afternoon of the day prior to his morning tea, his servants rowed out on a lotus lake in the royal garden and put a small handful of tea into the blossom of each lotus flower. They would then bind up the petals. As the tea dried overnight it would absorb the scent of the petals. The next morning the tea would be picked from the lake and offered to the king for his morning refreshment.

In Vietnam the tea ceremony is not elevated to a religious status as it is in Japan, but the preparation, serving and drinking of tea has great social significance. Drinking tea is an important ritual preliminary to conducting business. It is a customary practice to serve tea along with several items of food to the bride's family at the engagement party and is often given as a gift. It is served at marriage ceremonies and funerals.

When making tea for guests the tea is poured into a large cup called a 'cup-general' and from there is poured into smaller individual cups called 'soldier cups', ensuring an even distribution of flavour and colour.

Tea is often drunk in the many makeshift tea shops which also sell cakes and candies. Recently another kind of tea shop called *quan hong tra* (red tea shop) has begun to appear in major urban centres. They offer a kind of tea cocktail – a mix of tea with flower petals, sugar, honey or milk and grated ice which is blended until a froth appears then poured into a cup and served.

Tea has grown 'wild' in northern Vietnam for a very long time and is still harvested by the local people. In the late nineteenth century the French paid a lot of attention to growing tea and set up the first tea plantations, but the industry suffered from the continuous conflict in the area and only recently has tea production developed both for export and the domestic market. Today tea is cultivated in a number

Tea in Ben Thanh, Vietnam.

H'mong tea farmers in Vietnam (Oxfam Hong Kong is involved with Fairtrade tea production in e.g. Vietnam, mainland China and Hong Kong).

of provinces, including Thai Nguyen, where some of the best quality teas come from. Black tea is mainly exported. Green tea, on the other hand, is for local consumption, some of it scented with lotus.

Thailand also has a thriving tea industry. High quality tea is grown in the mountain areas especially for producing oolong tea. White tea, green tea and jasmine tea are also manufactured, but most of the tea grown is for internal consumption as the output is small.

The most popular tea drunk in Thailand is the sweet iced tea (served with or without milk) bought from small tea and coffee shops on the street, many of which have no seating areas. It usually comes in a small plastic bag with a straw as the tea is consumed 'on the go'.


## Along the Silk Road

Silk was the most important commodity traded along the Silk Road but many other precious and rare items were exchanged either from East to West or West to East, such as jade and lapis lazuli. Other 'exchanges' included the legendary 'heavenly' horses from the Ferghana valley, much needed for the Chinese armies, and flowers, vegetables, fruits, spices and tea.

At the eastern end of the Silk Road was the magnificent capital city of Changan (now Xian), and it was from here that the great trade caravans set out with their cargoes. The goods were usually carried on the backs of the Bactrian (two-humped) camel, often called 'ships of the desert'. The route took traders westward, travelling either north or south of the Taklamakan desert to Kashgar and then on to Kashmir, India, Afghanistan, Iran and such great cities as Samarkand, Baghdad and Constantinople (now Istanbul) and on to the Mediterranean.

The caravans stopped each night at strategically placed walled caravanserais (literally 'palaces of the caravans'), which were one day's journey apart to ensure everyone arrived by sunset. Caravanserais usually had a *chaikhana* (tea house), and the thought of a refreshing cup of tea at the end of a day's journey must have been very welcome for weary travellers.

It seems, however, that tea did not penetrate to western parts of Central Asia and beyond to the Mediterranean in any great quantities. Not many people or traders actually travelled the whole length of the Silk Road and the traders and merchants in what is now Iran and Afghanistan, who were literally 'middlemen', often controlled the carriage of goods over the middle section of the route and held a lucrative monopoly. The ancient city of Balkh in northern Afghanistan, which was once a thriving and important centre of trade before being destroyed by Genghis Khan in the twelfth century, seems to have been the western terminus of any major traffic in tea. Further west in Iran and the Middle East *qahwa* (coffee) was the preferred beverage and tea-drinking was to be adopted much later and arrived by other routes.

By the fourteenth and fifteenth centuries the opening up of safer and more lucrative sea routes to India and the Far

A *chaikhana* in Kabul, Afghanistan, 2009.

East led to the decline of the Silk Road as a major trading route to the West.

Many of the regions along the Silk Road share tea-drinking customs and traditions. Tea is drunk copiously and plays an essential role in hospitality and business dealings. One tradition is the drinking of three cups. Why three? There are many interpretations. Greg Mortenson's bestselling book *Three Cups of Tea* (2006) quotes Haji Ali, a chief of the remote village of Korphe in the Karakoram mountains in northern Pakistan: 'Here we drink three cups of tea to do business; the first you are a stranger, the second you become a friend, and the third, you join our family, and for our family we are prepared to do anything – even die.' A different meaning has been given by Louis Dupree in his encyclopaedic work *Afghanistan* (1973): 'The first cup assuages thirst, the second pledges friendship, the third is simply ostentatious.'

The same tradition is found in Morocco and other regions of North Africa. As people say in the Western Sahara,

The first glass is as sour as life
The second is as sweet as love
The third is as soft as death.

The explanation I like best is in Richard Trench's book *Forbidden Sands: A Search in the Sahara* (1980):

Three times he would go through these motions, three glasses and three brews for each person. Why three? I never found out. Once I asked Omar, but he just looked at me in disgust, shocked at my ignorance. 'Because it has always been so,' he said. I might just as well have asked him why the sun rose each morning.

A *chaikhana* in Samarkand; friends enjoy tea and flatbreads.

In many places tea is served with sugar lumps, which are placed on the tongue and the tea is drawn through them. Tea houses (*chaikhana*) are an important part of life in many countries along the Silk Road. They are places where men sit and relax enjoying tea, which is usually served from a constantly boiling samovar into individual teapots for each customer and poured into small porcelain cups or glasses.

Lady Macartney, who lived in the oasis city of Kashgar in Xinjiang from 1890 to 1918 as the wife of the British representative, wrote a charming and fascinating account of her life there. Here she describes a *chaikhana*:

Of course, the inevitable tea shop, or Chai-Khana, was everywhere, where people sat and drank tea while they listened to dreamy native music played by a band consisting of perhaps one or two long-necked mandolin-shaped instruments that produced very soft fairy-like music, accompanied by a small drum. Or they listened to a professional story teller . . . I suppose it was just this way that the Arabian Nights romances were first told.[3]

Kashgar was a major junction on the Silk Road and an important trading centre. Merchants and travellers would stop here for a rest, trade and take in fresh supplies for continuing on their arduous journeys. Lady Macartney extended her hospitality to many famous travellers and archaeologists, among them Sir Aurel Stein and Albert von Le Coq.

Kashgar lies at the heart of the Uyghur world. The Uyghurs are an ancient Turkic people who settled along the Silk Road in Central Asia, especially in Xinjiang province, a long time ago. They make tea in different ways: with salt and milk (*atkän çay*); with cream or sour cream and butter added to the tea in big bowls and served for a very nourishing breakfast; and black tea (*syn çay*) is often flavoured with cinnamon and served with sweets after a rich meal. Uyghurs living in the Ferghana valley prefer green tea called *kök çay*.

One of routes along the Silk Road leads to Kashmir, where tea is made in three different ways. *Kahwa* (also *qahwah or kehvi*) is the favourite and is often served on special occasions such as weddings and festivals. The exact origins of *kahwa* are unclear. Many Kashmiris believe that this drink dates back to the Yarkand Valley in Xinjiang during the time of the Kushan Empire in the first and second centuries AD. In Sir George Grierson's *A Dictionary of the Kashmiri Language* the word *kahwa* is defined: 'in Kashmiri, sweetened tea'.[4]

The word in Kashmir probably comes from the Turkish *kahve* (coffee), which in turn is derived from the Arabic word *qahwah*. In Arabic it means 'that which allows you to do without something', and is now the word for coffee in many countries of the Middle East. Coffee (*qahwah*) allows you to do without sleep; tea has similar properties. The tea, which is traditionally prepared in a samovar, is made by boiling green tea in water and adding cardamom, cinnamon, shredded almonds, saffron and sweetened with sugar or honey to taste. It is served in tiny, shallow cups called *khos*.

*Dabal chai* is made with green tea (often called *bambay chai* because it used to be imported via Bombay), sugar, cardamom, almonds and milk. *Sheer chai,* also known as *gulabi chai* (pink tea) or *nun chai*, is made with a special green or oolong tea. It is brewed over a fire and with the addition of salt, bicarbonate of soda and milk or cream makes a distinctly frothy and pink beverage. This tea is often served for breakfast.

A similar tea called *qymaq chai* (although sugar is usually added, not salt) is prepared in Afghanistan. *Qymaq chai* is made with green tea, flavoured with cardamom; with the addition of bicarbonate of soda and the process of aeration (by pouring the tea from a height from a pan to another pan several times), the tea turns dark red. Milk is added (and sugar too) and it becomes a pinkish colour. It has a strong, rich taste. *Qymaq*, a sort of clotted cream similar to the *kaymak* of the Middle East is floated on top of the tea.

*Qymaq chai* is elaborate to make and is served on formal occasions such as weddings and engagements. For everyday, both green and black tea (usually without milk but often flavoured with cardamom) is drunk from small porcelain cups or bowls or glasses called *istekhan*. Very often the custom is to drink the first cup or glass of tea with sugar *(chai shireen)*, continually topping up with more tea until the last cup is not sweet at all *(chai talkh)*. For guests an enormous amount of sugar is usually added – the more sugar, the more honour – and sweets are often an accompaniment, including sugared almonds called *noql*.

To the Kirghiz nomads in the very north-east, high up in the Wakkan corridor, tea is a luxury

A tea vendor in Afghanistan, *c.* 1970s.

worth so much that each camel driver carries it about his person in a beautifully embroidered little bag, which is cautiously produced to put tea in the kettle. Sugar is so precious that tea is drunk with salt not sugar, and salt is so scarce that it is only used in tea . . .[5]

Tea-drinking in Iran is quite recent and although it may have reached Persia from China by early caravans it made little impression. Coffee, which had arrived from Arabia in the ninth century, was the favoured drink for hundreds of years.

In the 1920s the former Shah's father became suspicious that coffee houses were fostering political dissent and decided to persuade people to switch to tea-drinking. He imported new strains of tea from China and recruited Chinese families to oversee and upgrade tea production in Iran. His efforts were successful and tea became the most popular beverage. Tea is grown around the Caspian Sea area but it is expensive and not enough is produced to satisfy the demand, so much of the tea is imported.

For formal entertaining, tea is sometimes flavoured with cinnamon or garnished with crushed rose petals.

# The Tea Road

Another caravan trading route out of China is the Tea Road, sometimes called the Great Tea Route. In 1689 the Treaty of Nerchinsk between Russia and China opened up this road. Starting in Kalgan in northern China the road went northward through the Gobi Desert, then west across the taiga of Siberia, arriving at the cosmopolitan centres of the Russian empire. Even though the journey was long and arduous (taking more than a year), this road became a major trading route.

Ladies around a samovar, painted *c.* 1860–75 by the Iranian artist Isma'il Jalayir.

High-ranking lamas during the tea ceremony, in their yurt attached to the temple, Ulan Bator, Mongolian People's Republic, 1962.

Furs and other goods were sent to China and traded for Chinese valuables, such as silks, medicinal plants (especially rhubarb) and tea.

The first samples of China tea are said to have been brought to Russia in 1616 by a Cossack called Tyumenets returning from a diplomatic mission to Mongolia. He reported that his mission 'drank warmed milk and butter, in it unknown leaves . . . '. Two years later, in 1618, a Chinese Embassy presented several chests of tea to the Russian court in Moscow. In 1638 the Mongol Khan sent 200 packets of tea as a precious gift to Tsar Mikhail Fedorovich. At that time very little was known in Russia about China and tea.

After the opening of the 'Tea Road' the amount of tea imported into Russia gradually increased. During the eighteenth century, especially during the reign of Catherine the Great (r. 1763-96), tea became fashionable among the Russian nobility and eventually spread to other classes.

Until the 1850s Russia imported loose leaf tea packed into chests. Later this was replaced by brick tea made in Russian factories in Hankou. When the Trans-Siberian Railway was completed at the beginning of the twentieth century the era of the camel caravan came to an end and tea was either transported by rail or shipped to the Black Sea port of Odessa. Tea plantations were established in Georgia at about the same time resulting in the spread of tea-drinking to all sectors of Russian society.

Russians evolved their own tea-drinking customs, the most important of which is the use of the samovar, meaning 'self-boiler' in Russian. The samovar is usually considered to be exclusively Russian but in fact it is used in the Central Asian states, Iran, Afghanistan, Kashmir and Turkey as well

A camel caravan on the move, packed with cases of tea, in a 1909 photograph.

A 1900s Russian samovar from Tula.

as other Slavic nations. Its origin is a matter of dispute. Some people believe it is of Oriental origin and suggest that Chinese and Korean vessels used for heating food were its forerunners. Other theories suggest that the ancestor of the samovar was a Chinese teapot that sat atop a brass charcoal burner or the Mongolian firepot which it resembles.

The samovar is a portable water heater traditionally made of brass (although some were made of silver and even gold). The water, which is poured into the reservoir, is heated by pine cones or charcoal fired through a central funnel. Boiling water is drawn off by means of a tap into a teapot containing tea leaves and then poured into porcelain cups or tea glasses.

Sometimes the tea is made very strong and kept warm by placing the teapot on top of the samovar. A little of this strong tea is poured into cups or glasses and then diluted with boiling water from the samovar.

Samovars were not produced in large numbers in Russia until the late eighteenth century. Tula, a long-established metal working centre south of Moscow, became the centre of manufacture.

Russian tea is usually served steaming hot, without milk, but perhaps with a slice of lemon, in traditional glasses held in elaborately crafted metal cupholders with handles. It is the custom to serve tea with something sweet, often a spoonful of fruit preserve.

From Russia the samovar and tea came to Turkey although tea was also imported by sea from the south east. Turkey is usually associated with coffee-drinking but Turks are also great tea-drinkers.

It is thought that originally tea was brought to Anatolia as early as the twelfth century. The earliest mention of tea in Turkish literature was in 1631 and comes from the pen of the famous Ottoman travel writer Evliya Çelebi. He mentions that the servants at the Custom Offices in Istanbul offer visiting officials of the Empire, beverages like coffee from Yemen, saleb[6] and tea.[7]

By the nineteenth century tea became important in the daily life of the Ottoman Turks. It was served in private homes and in public places – tea rooms and tea houses blossomed.

Sultan Abdulhamid II (1876–1909), although a coffee addict, showed keen interest in tea, especially its cultivation and realised its economic importance. Experiments in planting saplings and seeds were conducted in various parts of the Ottoman Empire and as they were brought from Russia (although originally a China tea) the tea was known

A Russian samovar and tea glasses.

as Moscow Tea. The eastern Black Sea coast area, which has a mild climate, high rainfall and fertile soil, proved to be ideal for growing tea. Unfortunately, due to troubled times and wars, cultivation was interrupted and it was not until the late 1930s that serious attempts were resumed. Atatürk, the founder of the Turkish Republic, encouraged home-grown tea as an alternative to imported coffee, which had become expensive and at times unavailable in the aftermath of the First World War. Turkey quickly became self-sufficient and in 1947 the Rize Tea Factory exported its first shipment abroad. Virtually all of the tea produced comes from the Rize province on the Black Sea coast, most of which is for domestic consumption. Today Turkey is the sixth largest tea producer in the world.

For those who do not have a samovar, a tea-kettle (*çaydan-lık*) is used. Water is boiled in the kettle and poured over tea leaves in a *demlik* (tea pot), which is then placed on top of the kettle, allowing the tea to brew. The tea can then be served light or strong according to taste. For most Turks the ideal is a transparent rich red. A little tea is poured from the *demlik* into tulip-shaped glasses called *ince belli*, or occasionally porcelain cups, and then diluted according to the desired strength with boiling water from the tea kettle. The glass is usually held by the rim in order to protect the drinker's fingers. The tea is often sweetened with sugar and sometimes served with a thin

Giant tea bags of freshly picked leaves wait to be collected by the tea factories of Rize, on Turkey's Black Sea coast.

Turkish tea served in tea glasses.

slice of lemon but never with milk. Serious tea-drinkers go
to a tea house where a samovar is kept constantly on the boil.

Traditional herbal teas, including those made with apple,
linden or lime blossom, rose hip and sage, are also popular.
Recently an 'apple tea' was introduced to the local market especially for tourists. It has nothing to do with traditional Turkish
tea. It is sweet, caffeine-free, slightly tart, with a mild apple
flavour. Interestingly the list of ingredients doesn't mention
apple, only sugar, citric acid, food essence and vitamin c.

## Mediterranean Shores

British traders in the Far East brought tea to Morocco in the
nineteenth century when the Crimean War forced them to
find new markets for their goods. Moroccans, who had been
making herbal infusions for centuries, took to drinking tea
enthusiastically but adapted it and made their own refreshing

infusion of green tea flavoured with fresh mint and plenty of sugar. (Spearmint, *Mentha viridis*, is considered not only the best but by many people as the only variety to be used.)

Preparation of the tea is considered an art and is steeped in ritual. The master of the house is usually responsible for the preparation and serving. It is traditionally made in a richly engraved silver pot to which he will add green tea. He then breaks off pieces of sugar from a cane sugar loaf and adds it to the pot with a handful of mint before pouring in boiling water and leaving to infuse for a few moments. The art is to pour the tea from a great height from the pot into small ornamental glasses in order to form a froth on the surface.

The drinking of green tea infused with mint spread from Morocco to Algeria, Tunisia, Libya and Egypt and to the nomadic tribes of Berbers and Tuareg in the Sahara. Black tea from India or Ceylon, made strong and sweet but without milk, is sometimes drunk, especially in Egypt, where tea-drinking has been important since the fifteenth century.

Arab women drinking tea in Casablanca, Morocco, *c.* 1910.

Moroccan tea is traditionally poured into decorative glasses from a height to form a froth on top.

A Tuareg man, offered tea inside a tent after heavy rain, pours it into a cup without looking. The photograph was taken in the Sahara desert outside Tomboctou, Mali.

In cafes tea is accompanied by a glass of cold water, a small glass of sugar, a spoon and occasionally a third glass containing mint.

Tea flavoured with mint is refreshing in hot climates and popular in other Arab countries including Iraq and the Gulf States. It is often the finale to an Arabian feast and helps aid digestion. Regional tastes vary and other herbs or spices may be used to flavour the tea including sage, cinnamon and dried limes. In the Gulf States Arabs welcome their guests with pitcher-shaped flasks filled with weak, delicate tea infused with saffron.

# 5

# Tea Comes to the West

When green tea from China was first imported into Europe in the seventeenth century it was considered a medicinal drink because of its bitter taste and its purported health-giving properties. The first printed reference to tea in European literature appeared in a book of travellers' tales compiled by a Venetian nobleman and geographer, Giambattista Ramusio, in 1559. One of the travellers, a Persian merchant named Hajji Mahommed, told Ramusio that the Chinese believed that

> one or two cups of this decoction taken on an empty stomach removes fever, headache, stomach ache, pain in the side or in the joints, and it should be taken as hot as you can bear it . . . And those people would gladly give a sack of rhubarb for an ounce of *Chai Catai*.[1]

In London in 1598 there appeared a translation of a Dutch work by the voyager and geographer Jan Huyghen van Linschoten. He wrote a detailed account of his voyage to the East Indies and describes how the Japanese drank tea and how much they prized the pots tea was drunk from:

Dutch painter Nicolaes Verkolje's 1710s oil painting of a tea party.

after their meat they use a certaine drinke, which is a pot with hote water, which they drinke as hote as ever they may indure, whether it be Winter or Summer . . . the afore-said warme water is made with the powder of a certaine hearbe called Chaa, which is much esteemed, and is well accounted of among them . . . for the pots wherein they sieth it, and wherein the hearbe is kept, with the earthen cups which they drinke it in, they esteeme as much of them, as we doe Diamants Rubies and other precious stones . . .[2]

The Portuguese, who were the first to circumnavigate the Cape of Good Hope, enjoyed a monopoly over Far Eastern trade in the sixteenth century, but had not paid much attention to trading in tea. It was their competitors the Dutch who brought the first shipment of both Japanese and China tea to

A 1740s German porcelain tea caddy.

Amsterdam in 1610. It was an expensive novelty but by 1660 tea was popular with those who could afford it. It was a high status beverage partly because of the expensive tea-set required to drink it. Well to do families even set aside special rooms where tea was prepared, served and drunk. 'The furniture consisted of tea-tables and chairs with cabinets for the cups and sugar boxes as well as for silver spoons and saffron pots . . . The tea and saffron were served together, the mixture being hot, sweetened and covered in a cup so as to preserve its aroma.'[3] Tea was an exotic and costly drink.

The Dutch marketed tea to other countries such as Germany, France and England. Tea arrived in Germany around 1640 and in 1709 the Germans discovered the secret of manufacturing china porcelain in Meissen. The designs of the tea services were based on Chinese models: the cups had no handles and were quite small; saucers were deep, more like a shallow bowl. At this time there was a vogue in aristocratic circles for anything Chinese. Many European princes and kings incorporated tea houses into their parks and gardens, one of the most splendid being Frederick the Great's Chinese tea house, built in 1756 at Sans Souci chateau in Potsdam. By the end of the eighteenth century, tea had become part of everyday life and had replaced the customary morning bowl of soup.

Today Germany is usually associated with coffee-drinking. However, the people of Friesland and East Friesland near the Dutch border are still enthusiastic tea-drinkers. They make their tea very strong, pour it over a sugar lump and add a thick layer of cream. Black tea from India or Sri Lanka is popular. It is interesting to note that Germany is a key buyer of the expensive first flush Darjeeling tea, importing about 50 per cent of the total Darjeeling output, and the main tea wholesalers in Europe are based in Hamburg. Some people predict that Germany could soon become Europe's largest tea-drinking nation.[4]

When tea arrived in France in the mid-seventeenth century it became a fashionable drink but because it was so costly it was mainly enjoyed in aristocratic circles. Louis XIV (1643–1715) of France was an early fan of tea, especially as a medicinal beverage, and drank it regularly to alleviate his symptoms of gout.

*Salons de Thé* became very popular in the early twentieth century:

> The golden age of the tea salon culminated in architecturally elaborate rooms of cream-colored boiserie, ornate mirrors, frescoed ceilings, crystal chandeliers, and marbled tables. They were splendid settings for the beau monde, who arrived in their carriages for 'le five o'clock.' Here, in

A 1760s French watercolour by 'Carmontelle' showing the Countess of Boufflers-Rouverel taking tea in her boudoir.

The Tea Room at Fauchon, Paris, 1910. The opening of Fauchon's 'Grand Salon de Thé' in 1898 was a memorable event; with it came the introduction of the 'Five o'clock Tea'.

a swirl of gay chatter, amid a spectacle of fancy pastries and a proliferation of teapots, the tea hour was celebrated.[5]

The *salon de thé* still thrives, especially in Paris. In the late 1980s the long established Mariage Frères Company, who were renowned as suppliers of the world's most exclusive teas, developed what has become known as 'French Tea', a refined approach to the tea-drinking ritual which includes precious green and white teas, new blends such as *Thé l'Opéra* (green tea flavoured with fruit and spices) and a tea-based cuisine including their famous tea-scented jellies. Mariage Frères today have three tea salons in Paris where their tea-loving customers can enjoy an exquisite afternoon tea with a choice of teas, mini sandwiches of foie gras, smoked salmon and prawns, cakes, scones, madeleines and a selection of patisseries from the '*Chariot Colonial*' in exotic and elegant surroundings.[6]

Across the channel in England the first tea arrived in about 1645. The first tea auction was held in London's Mincing Lane in 1656. Although its acceptance as a drink was slow, it was to last. Of the three new exotic drinks in seventeenth-century Europe – coffee, tea and chocolate – the British at first preferred coffee (perhaps because it was cheaper), and it was at the newly established coffee houses that tea was introduced to the public. In 1657 Thomas Garraway opened his coffee house in London and extolled the virtues of tea as being 'quite refined, which could be presented to princes and other great people'. Garraway also claimed that tea 'being prepared and drunk with milk and water it strengtheneth the inward parts' which suggests that in England milk was sometimes added to tea right from the beginning. Another early reference to milk in tea came from France via the pen of Madame de Sévigné. In a letter written in 1680 to a friend who was in poor health she advised her to drink milk and recommended that to avoid the cold milk clashing with the heat of the blood she should to add it to hot tea. She added that Mme de la Sablière recently took 'tea with her milk' because she liked it.

There is much debate about adding milk in tea and why this tradition started in the West. It has been suggested that milk was added to tea to prevent cracking delicate porcelain cups. Another question which is still hotly debated is whether milk should be added first to the cup or last. However, milk was not a common addition to tea in England before the 1720s. It was about this time that black tea overtook green tea in popularity and this could have played a part. Milk may have been added to offset the bitterness of the tea. Sugar was also added for the same reason.

In 1658 the first advertisement for tea appeared in an English newspaper. In 1660 Samuel Pepys wrote that he 'did

Advertisement by the United Kingdom Tea Company depicting Samuel Pepys, 1894.

A 1770s Scottish silver tea urn and a 1680s Scottish silver tea caddy.

send for a cup of tee, a China drink, of which I never had drunk before.' In 1662 Charles II married the Portuguese princess Catharine of Braganza. She was an early devotee of tea-drinking and her dowry included a chest of China tea. It is said that the first thing she asked for when she landed in Portsmouth was a cup of tea. She started serving it at Court and its popularity soon spread. In 1664 Charles II received a gift of tea from the East India Company. All fashionable society wanted to try the new drink but it was expensive and so remained, in those early days, a drink for the rich.

Not everyone knew what to do with this new exotic ingredient. It is said that the widow of the Duke of Monmouth (who was executed in 1685) sent a pound of tea to one of her relatives in Scotland without indicating how it was to be prepared. The cook boiled the tea leaves, threw away the water and served the leaves as a vegetable, like spinach.

In 1689 the East India Company started to import tea direct from China and in 1721 was given a monopoly on the tea trade. Historically and colloquially known as John Company, the East India Company was founded by the Royal Charter of Queen Elizabeth 1 in 1600. It became a powerful global economic force, the multinational conglomerate of its day. Although it was originally set up to trade in spices, the Company discovered many other lucrative products to be traded and by the end of the eighteenth century was making more money from the trade of tea than from anything else. To service this demand it built a fleet of high-capacity and beautiful sailing ships called 'East Indiamen' (sometimes called 'tea wagons'). The East Indiamen served well into the nineteenth century, by which time the tea trade had become important to other nations, especially America. The round trip from Europe to China and back again took almost two years and as long as the Company held a monopoly there was no urgency in bringing tea from China to Britain. However, in 1833 the Company lost its monopoly in the trade with China, which was mostly in tea, and the tea trade became virtually a free-for-all.

Merchants and sea captains raced to be the first to bring the new teas of the season to the West. This led to the development of new fast ships called clippers, the 'racing cars' of sailing ships. They had tall masts and huge sails and were sleeker than the East Indiamen. The most significant clippers were the China clippers, also called tea clippers, because their most important cargo was tea from China. Many had romantic names that hinted at speed, such as *Flying Cloud* and *Lightning*. Competition between American and British merchants led to the clipper races of the 1860s. The winner was the first ship to unload its cargo at the docks. The Great Tea Race of 1866 was the most famous. Twelve ships sailed from

Foochow to London. The breathtaking climax of this exciting race was reported in *The Times* of 12 September:

> The Ariel and Taeping, which had lost sight of each other for 70 days, found themselves on Wednesday morning at 8 o'clock, off the Lizard, running neck and neck up the Channel under every stitch of canvas that could be set, with a strong westerly wind. During the whole day the two ships kept their position, dashing up the Channel side by side in splendid style, sometimes almost on their beam ends, every sea sweeping their decks. On approaching the pilot station off Dungeness the next morning they each fired blue lights to signalize their position. At daybreak the pilots boarded them at the same moment, and the race was continued in the same exciting manner till they arrived in the Downs, where they both took steamtugs to tow them to the river. The ships had to shorten sail to enable

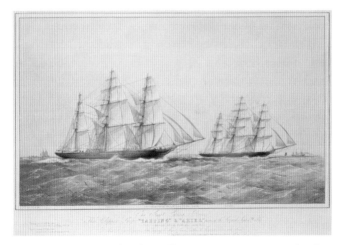

'The Great China Race: the Clipper Ships 'TAEPING & 'ARIEL passing the Lizard Sept 6th 1866 on their homeward voyage from Foo-Chow-Foo', an 1866 print by Thomas Goldsworth Dutton.

the tugs coming up and picking up the hawsers to take them in tow . . . both ships still neck and neck. The Taeping, however, was fortunate enough to have superiority in the power of steamtugs and reached Gravesend some time before the Ariel. The Serica followed closely upon them.

Clipper ships were sometimes called 'opium clippers' because opium was traded for tea with China, and it was this lucrative trade that enabled the shippers to invest in these new sleek ships. The main reason for the trade in opium was to balance trade with China. The Europeans desired silk, porcelain and tea from China but the Chinese did not want any European goods except silver, and not much of that. There was, however, a demand for opium in China despite the fact that it was an illegal drug, and it grew abundantly in British India. Trade was conducted in defiance of the Chinese authorities and in 1839 the Chinese Emperor decided to put a stop to it. A special Chinese commissioner was sent to Canton to eradicate the opium trade and confiscate all the foreigners' supplies of opium. Britain was outraged and what is called the 'Opium War' broke out.

The romantic era of the clipper ships came to an end when new steamships were developed and the Suez Canal opened in 1869. The Canal provided a short cut to the East but it was difficult for the clippers to manoeuvre in.

Until 1784 tea was heavily taxed and smuggling was rife. It was smuggled ashore from Dutch merchant ships anchored off the English coast. Underground passages led from caves to unfrequented roads, providing a nationwide distribution network. The smugglers were put out of business when Prime Minister William Pitt the Younger drastically cut the tax on tea from 119 per cent to 12.5 per cent and tea became affordable to all social classes.

An 1890s Horniman's Tea advertisement.

The high cost of tea also led to widespread adulteration. Very often what was sold as 'tea' was not tea at all, but elder leaves ash leaves or, most often, sloe leaves, boiled, baked, curled, dried and coloured until they resembled the best China green tea. Boiled with verdigris (copper acetate) and, when dry, painted with a toxic mixture of 'Dutch pink' dye and more verdigris, the 'tea' became poisonous. The same leaves were also converted into 'black tea' in much the same way except they were coloured with logwood, a dye from the West Indies.[7] When John Horniman set up a small business on the Isle of Wight in 1826 and, instead of selling loose tea, started packing it into sealed paper packets with a guaranteed net weight, the public reacted favourably. The system became general practice and helped put a stop to adulteration.

Not everyone liked tea and many were concerned about adulteration. Jonas Hanway in his essay of 1757 branded tea 'as pernicious to health, obstructing industry and impoverishing the nation'.

Dr Samuel Johnson, who was perhaps the most celebrated of all tea-drinkers, drinking, it is said, 25 cups a day, came to tea's defence and in the words of Osbert Lancaster:

> In a series of shattering broadsides in the *Literary Magazine* Dr Johnson utterly demolished the absurd pretensions of Mr Hanway and proudly ran up his flag as the unswerving addict and champion of tea, calling himself 'A hardened and shameless tea-drinker who has for many years diluted his meals with only the infusion of this fascinating plant; whose kettle has scarcely time to cool; who with tea amuses the evening, with tea solaces the midnight – and with tea welcomes the morning.'

Dr Johnson was known to frequent London's famed coffee houses. Gentlemen went there to discuss the politics and business of the day over a cup of coffee or tea. Coffee houses were smoky, noisy places and by the early eighteenth century had become disreputable. Women were not allowed to enter (although women often did the serving) and in case any no gentlewoman would have cared to set foot in one.

Ladies therefore took their tea at home and because it was so expensive they kept the tea in their boudoir or drawing room. At first they used a Chinese jar or bottle called a teapoy or catty (a word meaning a Malayan weight of approximately 21 ounces). This later came to be called a caddy, which evolved into a casket made of wood, tortoiseshell, papier mâché or silver with a lock and key.

A 1786 print by Thomas Rowlandson of Dr Johnson taking tea with Mrs Boswell in the Highlands.

H.C. Fecit

A Frenchman not aware of the custom, c
which being immediately replenished b
politeness to drink the contents which
until he perceived the Lady pouring out
Ah! Madame, excuse me I can take

French Politeness.

Pub.d Sep.r 1795 by G. Humphrey 26 S.t James's Street

...urned his cup without the spoon in it —
...f the house, he thought it a point of
... to do, to the great surprise of the company
... when he rose in great agony and cried

By the middle of the eighteenth century tea-drinking had spread to the middle classes and replaced ale for breakfast and gin at other times of the day. As coffee-drinking declined tea became Britain's most popular beverage. It was not the cost which caused coffee's decline. Tea was more expensive per pound, although this was compensated for by the smaller amount required to brew the tea.[8] A possible explanation is that to brew tea is easier, all that is needed is boiling water; coffee, in contrast, requires roasting, grinding and brewing. This could be done in the coffee houses but not so easily at home.[9] The manner of trading may also have played a part. The tea trade was controlled by the powerful East India Company, whereas the coffee trade was run by independent merchants.

As coffee houses declined, the pleasure gardens of London turned into tea gardens. They became the place to go, to see and to be seen. Among these were Marylebone, Vauxhall and Ranelagh, which provided outdoor entertainment for Londoners of every class. The attractions included music, conjurors, acrobats, fireworks, riding, bowling and boat trips as well as refreshments and tea.

Fashions change, and with the expansion of London in the early nineteenth century the tea gardens closed down. Tea-drinking became confined to the home. Great social changes were also taking place. The main meal of dinner, previously taken in the middle of the afternoon, shifted to much later in the evening, sometimes as late as 8 or 9 o'clock, and only a light lunch was taken midday. Anna Maria, the Seventh Duchess of Bedford, is said to have experienced 'a sinking feeling' in the middle of the afternoon during the

*previous*: The dangers of not knowing correct etiquette. Robert Cruikshank's 1825 cartoon 'A Tea Party – or English Manners and French Politeness'.

A 19th-century Chinese porcelain tea bowl.

long gap between luncheon and dinner. She started taking a pot of tea with some light refreshments in her room mid-afternoon. She then began to have tea sent to her boudoir for herself and guests. In addition to a selection of teas (both China and Indian – the first Indian tea arrived in 1839 and Ceylon teas soon after in 1879), the Duchess served toast and fine breads. The tradition of afternoon tea was born.

By the 1850s afternoon tea began to be served in the drawing room and became more elaborate and the focus for social visits. Dainty sandwiches, biscuits, cakes and pastries were served. The portions were usually small – just enough to stave off hunger pangs until dinner time. In winter, teas such as Assam with its rich pungent flavour and warming foods such as cinnamon toast, hot buttered crumpets and rich fruit cakes might be served round the fireside; in summer, delicate Earl

Grey or the golden taste of Ceylon accompanied cucumber sandwiches and scones with strawberries and cream.

Elegant tea-ware in silver or fine bone china, cake stands, sandwich trays, sugar tongs and tea strainers were the height of fashion. Tables were laid with embroidered or lace cloths and serviettes. Afternoon tea became a special occasion.

In wealthy Victorian homes children had their own special nursery teas, usually at four or five o' clock. There would be sandwiches, perhaps some boiled eggs with 'soldiers' (fingers of bread and butter), and a variety of sweet things such as muffins, small cakes, buns or biscuits.

Children enjoying afternoon tea in an ominously worded tea advertisement of the 1890s.

**BREAKFAST AND TEA CHINA.**

4 Tea Cups... 2 Bread and Butter Plates... 1 Teapot... 1 Butter Dish... 1 Sardine Box... 2 Coffee Cups...
Afternoon Tea Set... 1 Milk Jug... 1 Jug... 1 Bread Dish... 1 Bacon Dish... 1 Marmalade Jar... 4 Breakfast Cups...

Breakfast and tea china, including tea cups, bread and butter plates and a teapot.

Other tea time rituals became fashionable, including 'At Home' teas and 'Tea Receptions'. These were large events which took place in the afternoons for up to two hundred guests. Servants would pour and hand round cups of tea, sugar, cream or milk, cakes and bread and butter. On these occasions some form of musical entertainment might be provided. There were also bridge teas, tennis teas, farmhouse teas, picnic teas, cream teas and so on.

In contrast to these elegant teas, the tradition of high tea was finding a place in lower and middle class homes at about the same time. The price of tea had fallen after the Commutation Act of 1784 and by the mid-nineteenth century cheaper Indian tea was imported into Britain. Working-class families were now able to afford to drink tea as their main beverage and, returning home from the mines and factories, welcomed a good hearty meal at about six o'clock which often included hot dishes such as Welsh rarebit or kippers. Bread and butter would accompany cold meats, pies, cheeses, cakes, fruit loaves and preserves, all served with a large pot of strong black tea with milk and sugar.

When a resourceful manageress of the Aerated Bread Company (ABC), a chain of bakery shops, persuaded the firm's directors in 1864 to open up a room at the back of the store to the public for tea and refreshments the tea room was born. The venture proved popular, not just with ladies of high society but with shop assistants, office workers and ordinary shoppers. Going out to tea became the new fashion. Women could go unaccompanied to meet their friends.

In Scotland Glaswegians were introduced to the delights of the tea room in 1875 when Stuart Cranston, an enterprising and adventurous young tea dealer who owned a small retail tea business in Glasgow, decided to serve cups of tea with bread and butter and cakes on the premises. Cranston, who had

Miss Cranston's tea rooms in Buchanan Street, Glasgow, boast an 1897 Mackintosh mural.

strong family connections with the Temperance Movement, saw that working people needed somewhere to take refreshments during the day and the idea that tea was 'the cup that cheers but not inebriates' certainly influenced him.[10] He also thought his customers, both men and women, might like to taste teas in comfort before buying so he provided tables for sixteen customers 'elbow to elbow' at his shop at 2 Queen Street. He advertised a cup of China tea 'with sugar and cream, for 2d bread and cakes extra'.

In 1878 Cranston's sister Kate opened her own tea rooms and in 1897 she commissioned the 28-year-old architect Charles Rennie Mackintosh to decorate her third establishment with Art Nouveau murals. Over the next two decades

A 'nippy' serves tea at Lyon's tea shop in London's Piccadilly.

he designed for her, with dazzling artistic inventiveness, several tearooms including not only murals but structure, furniture, even the waitresses' dresses. It was the 'new art' interior and what might be called 'designer' tea rooms which made Miss Cranston's tea rooms internationally renowned. Her famous Willow Tea Rooms on fashionable Sauchiehall Street in Glasgow opened in November 1903 and were the very epitome of chic.

The dynamic catering entrepreneur Joseph Lyons opened his first London tea room in 1894 at 213 Piccadilly and more followed. They proved highly successful, providing good cheap food with smartness and cleanliness. The waitresses became so famous for their speed and efficiency that they were called 'nippies'.

Another entrepreneur, originally from Switzerland and who, on becoming an English citizen, changed his name from

Afternoon tea at Bettys Café Tea Rooms, Harrogate.

Fritz Bützer to Frederick Belmont, opened his first Bettys cafe on 17 July 1919 in Harrogate, Yorkshire. It was exquisitely decorated and fitted out with showcases in precious wood and mirrors and glass on the walls. More Bettys followed in other towns of Yorkshire.

Going out to tea in England, on the Continent and in the USA reached its heyday in Edwardian times. Afternoon teas were served in the lounges and palm courts of exclusive hotels to musical accompaniment. In 1913 these stylish teas took on a new slant with the arrival of the exotic and risqué dance craze from Argentina, the tango. Tea and tango came together and created a new fashion, the tea dance or *Thé Dansant*. Gladys Crozier, a society hostess and leading authority on tea dancing, described the scene in 1913:

> What could be pleasanter, for instance, on a dull wintry afternoon, at five o'clock or so, when calls or shopping

are over, than to drop in to one of the cheery little 'Thé Dansant' clubs, which have sprung up all over the West End . . . to take one's place at a tiny table . . . to enjoy a most elaborate and delicious tea . . . whilst listening to an excellent string band (and) . . . joining in the dance . . . [11]

The craze for tea dances lasted into the early 1920s, when they were replaced by the cocktail party.

In contrast to these exotic and stylish teas tea-drinking became a great morale booster during the Second World War. Although rationed, tea was cheap. Troops in camps called their strong early morning tea 'gunfire'.

In the 1950s tea-drinking at tea shops declined, perhaps because of the popularity of the newly fashionable coffee bars,

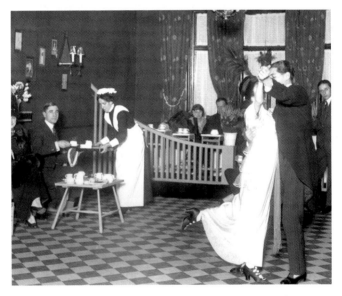

'Tea and Tango – Tango Becomes the Rage', 1914. Tea is served at a tango exhibition at the Argentine and Brazilian Dancing Salon in London demonstrated by Senor Marquis and Gladys Clayton.

Volunteers of the WRVS serving tea to British civilians during the Second World War.

but it enjoyed a renaissance in the 1970s when the National Trust started to offer visitors to their historic properties a traditional afternoon tea. A new and stylish independent venture was Jane Pettigrew's shop, Tea-Time, which opened in Clapham, London in 1983. Its 1930s art deco theme made it popular with visitors from all over London and even further afield. Today tea rooms flourish all over Britain. In London hotels such as the Ritz and the Dorchester are still renowned for their elegant afternoon teas. The author recently enjoyed tea at the Dorchester where she was served delicate finger sandwiches, scones with jam and cream, dainty cakes, a choice of speciality teas and a glass of champagne, all to piano accompaniment.

Plucking tea on the Tregothnan Estate, Cornwall.

In 1989 the first tea plantation in the United Kingdom was established on the Tregothnan Estate in Cornwall. They produce black and green teas for blending with other teas, many of which are being exported to the tea-loving Japanese.

## North America

The United States is usually associated with coffee-drinking. Tea was, however, the favoured drink of the colonists in the seventeenth and eighteenth centuries until the tax imposed on it sparked off the Revolutionary War in 1775.

The Dutch introduced tea to their trading post, New Amsterdam, in the 1650s, not long after the drink had arrived in Europe. They brought their own customs of tea-drinking.

Tea was made with saffron water or flavoured with peach leaves, and ladies gave tea parties using tiny teacups imported from China.

In 1664 British colonists conquered the settlement, which they renamed New York. The East India Company now supplied the settlers with tea. Tea was expensive but by the 1750s tea-drinking had become established among the wealthy and gradually started to filter down to households of modest means.

New York had impressive tea gardens fashioned after those of London's Vauxhall and Ranelagh Gardens. The Tea Water Pump Garden became famous for providing water from a spring which was used for making tea. At that time the water in New York was notoriously bad and other springs located on the city's outskirts led to a thriving tea-water trade. Special tea-water pumps were constructed over the springs and vendors would hawk this water throughout the city.

The long journey from China to New York via London was a profitable one for the East India Company and tea became a convenient product for the British to tax heavily. A high duty on tea had to be paid in London even before it was shipped across the Atlantic to America. In 1765 the British Government imposed the Stamp Tax largely to pay for the recent costly wars against the French and the Native Americans. This immediately caused riots and a boycott of British goods, forcing the British government to back down and withdraw the tax. However, in 1767 a new levy was imposed on American imports of four commodities: paper, glass, lead and tea. This caused a further storm of protests by the colonists, forcing the British government once again to abandon the duties. They did, except for tea, which was to be taxed 3d. for each pound. Instead of paying it, the colonists either boycotted tea altogether or simply smuggled it in from Holland. The East

India Company as a result found itself with large stocks of surplus tea and faced bankruptcy. So, with the help of Parliament, they secured the 1773 Tea Act, which allowed them to ship tea to America direct without payment of English duty.

This meant that tea was now cheaper than even the smuggled tea despite the fact that the tax of 3d. per pound was still included in the price! However, by this time tea had become the symbol of revolutionary action. If the colonies paid the tax on tea they would be acknowledging Parliament's right to tax them. It was assumed by the British government that the colonists would rather pay the tax than deny themselves the pleasure of a cup of tea. They were wrong. Tea consumption plummeted and patriots took to drinking 'liberty tea' made from the leaves of loosestrife (a wild flower) or raspberry leaves, chamomile and sage. Some turned to drinking coffee. A group called The Sons of Liberty declared no tea should be allowed to be unloaded at the docks and that those who attempted to do so would be considered the enemies of the country.

Boston had from the very beginning been a centre of American resistance to British rule and when three English ships sailed into the harbour in late November 1773, they were not allowed to discharge their cargo of tea. However, they were also under orders not to sail without discharging their holds completely. This deadlock was settled on the night of 16 December 1773 when, under cover of darkness, a group of colonists disguised as 'Indians' boarded the ships and threw 342 chests of tea overboard into the harbour. George Hewes was a member of the group and his recollection was published some years later:

> When we arrived at the wharf . . . they divided us into
> three parties, for the purpose of boarding the three
> ships which contained the tea . . . ordered me to go to

the captain and demand of him the keys to the hatches and a dozen candles . . . [he] delivered the articles; but requested me . . . to do no damage to the ship or rigging. We then were ordered by our commander to open the hatches and take out all the chests of tea and throw them overboard . . . first cutting and splitting the chests with our tomahawks, so as thoroughly to expose them to the effects of the water.

In about three hours from the time we went on board, we had thus broken and thrown overboard every tea chest to be found in the ship, while those in the other ships were disposing of the tea in the same way . . . We were surrounded by British armed ships, but no attempt was made to resist us.[12]

This event, which became known as the Boston Tea Party, ultimately sparked off the War of Independence. Tea, having been the favourite beverage, became a hated symbol of oppression. Americans took to drinking coffee.

*The Destruction of Tea at Boston Harbor,* an 1840s popular print of the Boston Tea Party.

*The Cup of Tea*, an 1880s oil painting by Mary Cassatt.

It wasn't until after the American Revolution that tea consumption revived. In the late 1800s American ladies were gathering in their parlours and partaking of 'low tea', often to raise funds for their churches or charities. (Afternoon tea was often called 'low tea' because it was usually served on low

A 1910 caricature of American suffragettes having a tea party in jail.

tables which were placed near sofas or chairs in a sitting room. The meal called 'high tea', which was a much more substantial meal, was eaten at a high dining table.) In the early twentieth century the custom of taking afternoon tea spread to tea rooms, department stores and hotels. Tea rooms, which were run by women, were popular during the 1920s, a decade when alcoholic beverages were outlawed, thus encouraging people to drink tea and coffee in public instead. The Depression and the end of Prohibition in the 1930s saw a decline in tea rooms but by the 1990s they experienced a revival. Today San Francisco, for example, boasts many tea rooms, including the Secret Garden, which serves traditional 'afternoon tea', and the Samovar Tea Lounge, which serves more exotic fare such as a Moorish platter with mint tea or Russian Chay platter with Samovar black tea.

Elegant 'afternoon teas' were served at places like New York's Plaza Hotel, which opened in 1907, and Boston's Ritz-Carlton in 1927. Both gained a reputation for serving stylish teas which continues to this day. As in Europe, late afternoon tea dances became all the rage and continued up until the Second World War. Tea dances, like the tea gardens of earlier years, provided an opportunity for young men and women to socialize without damaging their reputations.

Lillian Russell, the famous American actress, wrote in her column in the *Chicago Daily Tribune* on 13 February 1914: 'What is this new craze which has cast a spell over the universe? What is the attraction of the afternoon tea?' She concludes:

> How much better for a woman to spend the afternoon in dancing than in leaning over the bridge table gambling . . . Now she can join her friends at the *thé dansant*, and after her husband leaves his office he meets here there, and

Eliel Saarinen, prototype tea service, *c.* 1933–5, electroplated nickel silver, brass and bakelite.

Iced tea.

after one or two dances they speed homeward together
after a day pleasantly and satisfactorily spent.

Iced tea must have been an ideal refreshment for people
enjoying *thé dansant*. Some sources suggest that Americans
began putting ice into their tea around 1860. However, the
'invention' of iced tea is credited to an English tea merchant,
Richard Blechynden. He was in charge of a special tea pavilion at the 1904 St Louis World's Trade Fair popularizing
black teas from India and Ceylon. It was proving difficult to
sell hot cups of tea to the fairgoers in the sweltering heat so

he came up with the inspired idea of pouring the hot tea over ice in cups. Customers were soon crowding around to buy the new cool beverage. Today more than 80 per cent of all tea consumed in the US is served over ice. Iced tea is particularly popular in the South and what is called 'hot tea' is often prepared by heating up iced tea. In fact, if you order 'tea' in the US you will automatically be served iced tea. 'Sun tea' is tea steeped in cold water, left to stand in the sun for several hours, and then iced. Instant iced tea was introduced in 1953 under the label 'White Rose Redi-Tea' by the Seeman Brothers of New York City.

Not long after the World's Fair in 1908 another invention was in the making, this one quite by accident. Thomas Sullivan, a New York City tea importer started sending his customers samples of tea in hand-sewn silk bags instead of the usual tins, which was cheaper. To his surprise some of his customers assumed that the bags were to be used in the same manner as metal infusers and put the bags into the pot. The idea caught on. The easy-to-use bags revolutionized the tea industry. The centuries-old rituals of teamaking had been turned into a quick and easy convenience. Silk was subsequently replaced by gauze. Modern tea bags are usually made of paper fibre. However, for environmental reasons silk tea bags are making a comeback and those made from corn-starch are also seen as being eco-friendly. They can also be made of nylon or other synthetic material.

Lipton Teas in the USA were the first to use printed tags with brewing instructions and in 1952 patented the first major tea bag innovation for many years: the four-sided, double chamber 'flo-thru' tea bag, which enabled a faster and superior infusion. Britain was slow to adopt the use of tea bags and it was not until the 1950s that they took off, but by 2007 tea bags made up a remarkable 96 per cent of the British market. Tetleys launched their tea bag in 1953 and has continued to design new ones. Aside from the drawstring tea bag where the bag has two strings for easy wringing, Tetleys also designed the round tea bag. Liptons developed a pyramid shaped tea bag which contains high quality full-leaf teas. Some tea bags have an attached piece of string with a tag which assists in removing the bag while also identifying the type of tea. Empty tea bags are now also available, enabling the tea drinker to fill them with tea leaves of their choice. These are typically an open-ended pouch with a long flap. The pouch is filled with the leaf tea and the flap closed into the pouch to retain the tea. Similarly, tea 'socks' or 'nets' made from cotton have also become popular. They have the advantage that they can be washed and reused.

Two new tea-drinking trends also emerged in the 1990s: bubble tea, which originated in Taiwan (see page 57), and 'chai'. Chai is similar to the *masala chai* of India where it originated and is used loosely as a term to denote tea with spices, sweeteners and milk, which can be served hot or cold. Chai may have been introduced in coffee houses in Boulder and Portland in the 1960s by young counterculture travellers returning from their treks in India and Nepal.

In the mid-1990s several companies began marketing chai concentrates. Starbucks, which has sold spiced tea bags since 1995, began serving hot and cold chai latte in its stores. Chai latte is a version of the café latte, the tea being flavoured with a spiced tea concentrate, with cream or condensed milk, frothed in an espresso machine and topped with whipped cream.

Tea-drinking is undergoing a revival in the United States. Annual sales have grown from less than $1 billion before 1990 to an estimated $6 billion in 2009 and are projected to exceed $10 billion by 2011. The most dynamic growth is in

A modern tea doll
from Labrador,
Canada.

so-called 'specialty' teas, which include organic, fair-trade and origin-specific (country and estate) teas.

In Canada, where there are large communities from Asia, 'hot' tea is favoured over iced tea, although the climate may have played a part in this.

Tea was amongst the early supplies taken to Canada by the Hudson Bay Company and became popular not just with trappers but also First Nations and Inuit, who still drink their tea very strong and without milk or sugar and regard it as a very precious drink. Prior to the 1950s, the Labrador Innu bands were migratory. When the Innu people of Sheshatsui, Labrador travelled to the hunting grounds, everyone was expected to carry his or her share of the load. The children carried theirs by bringing along a doll that held a reserve of around two pounds of loose tea stuffed in its body. When the camp was set up and the tea was needed to provide a warm drink, it was removed. The doll could be re-stuffed with grass or leaves.

Today tea rooms are flourishing all over the country. The most famous tea room for many decades is the Victoria Room in the Empress Hotel in Victoria. Traditional English afternoon tea is still served today in elegant surroundings. As a memento a tin of the special Empress' own loose tea is also presented to the customer.

# Australia

At the other side of the world, Australians were the greatest black tea-drinkers at the beginning of the twentieth century. The traditional way of making tea in the outback is in a billy can, a kind of simple tin with a metal wire handle. A fire is lit and a tripod constructed to hang the 'billy' from. The billy is then filled with water from a nearby creek and brought to the boil. Tea is added and traditionally a gum leaf included for extra flavour. The tea is made quite strong and, after steeping, in order to settle the tea leaves to the bottom the billy is swung back and forth at arm's length or swung round the head three times. This requires some level of caution. The tea is then poured into tin mugs and, as fresh milk and sugar are probably not available when camping in the outback, sweetened condensed milk is added, making an invigorating brew.

*Stockmen's Rest*: two stockmen take a break for a cup of billy tea in the Australian outback in a contemporary oil by Robert Todonai.

In 1881 Scotsman James Inglis started the Billy Tea Company, decorating the packet with a line-drawing of a swagman boiling his billy can by his campfire. In 1902 he bought the rights to the famous song 'Waltzing Matilda', which had been written in 1895 by Andrew Barton 'Banjo' Paterson to use as an advertising jingle.

> Once a jolly swagman camped by a billabong
> Under the shade of a coolibah tree,
> And he sang as he watched and waited 'til his billy boiled
> 'You'll come a-Waltzing Matilda, with me.'[13]

Australia still likes its old-style 'Billy Tea', which is often sold in grocery stores in silver billy cans.

# 6

# India, Sri Lanka and Indonesia

Tea consumption in north-eastern India probably dates back many centuries but not as the sort of drink we know. The hill tribes of this region (including Burma and Thailand) were using the wild tea plant to make a kind of pickled or fermented tea called *miang* or *lephet*. In the Himalayan regions tea was also drunk as a kind of thick soup similar to the butter tea of Tibet.

Dutch merchants first brought China tea to India early in the seventeenth century and it quickly became popular, although at that time it was considered a medicinal drink. Albert Mandelslo, a gentleman of the court of Holstein who visited the English trading post on the west coast at Surat in 1638, recorded:

> At our ordinary meetings every day we took only *Thé*, which is commonly used all over the *Indies*, not only among those of the country, but also among the *Dutch* and the *English*, who take it as a drug that cleanses the stomach, and digests the superfluous humours, by a temperate heat particular thereto.[1]

The Reverend John Ovington, who was chaplain at Surat between 1689 and 1693, was an early enthusiast of tea drinking. In his book *Voyage to Surat in the Year 1689*, he records:

> Tea likewise is a common Drink with all the Inhabitants of *India*, as well *Europeans* as Natives; and by the *Dutch* is used as such a standing Entertainment, that the Tea-pot's seldom off the Fire, or unimploy'd.

He also explains how the Banians, members of a trading caste took their tea:

> with some hot Spice intermixt and boiled in the Water, [it] has the Repute of prevailing against the Headach, Gravel, and Griping in the Guts, and 'tis generally drunk in *India*, either with sugar-Candy, or, by the more curious, with some Conserv'd Lemons.

After his return to England Ovington did much to popularise tea by means of an essay he wrote in 1699: *An Essay upon the Nature of Qualities of Tea*.

But both Mandelslo and Ovington were mistaken in their assumption that tea was a common drink in India. It was not until the mid-nineteenth century that the British discovered that the tea plant was indigenous to north-east India as well as to China and it was not until the mid-twentieth century that tea became a drink for the masses in India.

As early as 1774 the East India Company was exploring the possibilities of growing tea in other countries apart from China and sent a few seeds to the British emissary in Bhutan to plant there. Several years later Sir Joseph Banks, the famous British naturalist, was engaged to recommend crops to the East India Company that might be grown for profit and he suggested tea. However, little was done for nearly fifty years.

It was a Scottish major called Robert Bruce who, while working in Assam in 1823, noticed that the inhabitants were making tea from a plant which looked similar to the Chinese *Camellia sinensis*. (It was the Assam variety.) There was much confusion about the tea plant. The English thought black and green tea came from two different species and dubbed the indigenous Indian plant Bohea (a black Chinese tea). The two plants differ in that the Chinese plant has smaller leaves than the Indian.

Robert Bruce died in 1824 but not before he had told his brother Charles about his discovery and had sent him some seeds. Charles arranged for some of these plants to be cultivated in the botanical gardens of Calcutta. Convinced that this was tea, he informed the government in 1832.

In the 1830s the British East India Company became concerned that they might lose the monopoly of the China trade. There was a great demand for tea in Britain and it was in her interests that tea cultivation be established in India. In 1834 the Company was indeed stripped of its monopoly and a Tea Committee was set up. A plan was developed to introduce tea culture into India. Opinions were divided as to whether the Chinese tea plants or the Assam variety should be cultivated. Some insisted that only the China plants were good enough for commercial production and that native plants would yield an inferior tea. Others favoured cultivating the Assam tea plant which would be much better suited to local conditions.

Many mistakes were made. China plants were chosen for experimental plots but then there was disagreement about where they should be planted. The plants imported from China fared badly. Some died on the way, others were planted in poor soil, but a few survived. Another mistake was bringing in Chinese workers to work on the plots. The English assumed that all Chinese people would know about growing and producing tea, which of course was not the case. Many knew nothing about tea. However, despite these problems the first black tea produced from Chinese plants was processed and several tea chests were shipped to London and delivered in 1838. The consignment was auctioned at India House in January 1839. The Assam Tea Company was formed in 1840 and established its own plantations in Assam.

Although tea was much consumed in Europe and America very little was known about it and in an attempt to learn more a Scottish botanist called Robert Fortune was sent to China in 1842. In 1848 he was sent again by the East India Company specifically to obtain the finest tea plants to be grown. At that time travel for Europeans within China was much restricted by the Chinese government and it was forbidden for anyone to purchase tea plants. Fortune, who had become well acquainted with China, the people and the language, managed to penetrate the tea-growing areas by travelling in disguise. It was an early instance of industrial espionage and he managed to smuggle out a large quantity of seed and 20,000 seedlings to the East India Company's Himalayan plantations.

Fortune's book *A Journey to the Tea Countries of China* in 1852 gives an account of his quest and adventures. Here he describes how a Taoist priest who had given him hospitality gives him some tea plants, much to his delight:

> He went out to his tea plantations and brought me some young plants which he begged me to accept. I felt highly pleased . . . and gladly accepted the plants, which increased my store very considerably; these with the other plants were carefully packed with their roots in damp moss, and the whole package was then covered with oil-paper. The

Tea plantations view in the green tea district of China, mid-19th century, from Robert Fortune's 1852 book *A Journey to the Tea Countries of China.*

latter precaution was taken to screen them from the sun, and also from the prying eyes of the Chinese . . .

Both Chinese tea plants and the local Assam variety were cultivated but the Assam plants proved more successful and gradually took over. In the 1860s tea plantations were developed in other parts of India, notably Darjeeling. Tea mania struck and entrepreneurs scrambled to set up tea plantations in order to make their fortunes. But it was not until the 1870s that the tea industry in India stabilized and finally began producing good-quality tea at a profit, and tea-drinking by the British in India got under way. It was drunk in the same way as it is today in Britain, with milk and sugar (in India the sugar might be in the form of jaggery or date palm sugar). Sometimes spices and other ingredients were added. Beatrice Vieyra in her book *Culinary Art Sparklets*, published in India in 1904, gives a recipe for Cutchee Tea that includes not only milk and sugar but almonds, sago, cardamom pods and rosewater.

During the nineteenth century many British women travelled to India, often in search of husbands. They brought with them the tradition of afternoon tea, which became embedded in colonial life. It was usually served after tiffin. (Tiffin is an Anglo-Indian term used in parts of India to mean lunch, but it can also mean a light snack in the middle of the day or in the afternoon.) Flora Annie Steel describes a typical Anglo-Indian tea in her book *The Complete Indian Housekeeper and Cook* (1888): 'In regard to eatables, plain bread and butter should invariably be a standing dish. Many people do not care for cakes, and yet find a cup of tea or coffee better for something to eat with it.'

In Indian cities and at hill stations the British set up exclusive clubs centred on sports, the bar and the dining room.

Afternoon tea in British India.

Afternoon tea was served in wood-panelled rooms, on shady verandas, or out on manicured lawns accompanied by typical Anglo-Indian fare such as club sandwiches, toasts grilled with toppings of garlic, green chillies and grated cheese, and, always, spicy pakoras, samosas and English cakes. Tea planters established clubs too, like the Darjeeling Club and High Range Club in Munnar.[2]

In British India the day began early, often before dawn with *chota hazri* ('little breakfast'), sometimes called 'bed tea'. Servants brought an early morning pot or cup of tea with milk and sugar and perhaps some fruit or a biscuit for their employers, often administrators or army officers, who liked to work in the cool period before sunrise. For travellers on Indian trains *chota hazri* became an established custom, as it did with those who went riding before the main breakfast, which was served at about 9 or 10 o'clock.

Tea-drinking was strongly associated with the British in India but for the Indian population tea was too expensive and tea-drinking was slow to be taken up. In 1881 the Tea Association of India was set up to formulate policies for the development and growth of the tea industry, but it wasn't

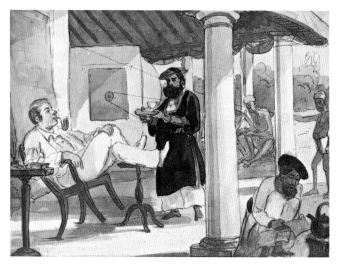

'Our Colonel' taking tea on the veranda, in one of Captain G. F. Atkinson's illustrations to his 1859 memoir of social life at 'Our Station' in India.

until 1901 that they realized that there was potentially a large market for tea in India. They set up a marketing campaign by employing a superintendent and two 'smart European travellers' to visit grocers and persuade them to stock more tea. This early campaign was not very successful and it was not until the First World War that the campaign began to gain momentum and to show some signs of success. Tea stalls were set up in factories, coal mines and cotton mills and workers were allowed tea breaks. On the Indian Railways, the Tea Association equipped small contractors with kettles and cups and packets of tea and set them to work at the major railway junctions in the Punjab, the North-West Frontier and Bengal. Tea vendors would call out '*Char! Gurram, gurram char!*' 'Tea hot, hot tea!' as they walked down the platform. The first thing rail passengers hear on waking up on a train in northern India is the *chai wallah*, calling out 'chai, chai, chai' as he strides through the carriages with his kettle swinging in one hand and glasses in the other.[3]

Tea shops were set up in the large towns, cities and ports. But it was not until the 1950s that tea became the drink of the masses. Today tea is a normal part of everyday life of India. It is brewed at railway stations, bus stations, bazaars, offices and sold by the *chai mallahs*, who usually do not have much more than a simple table, perhaps a rickety chair or bench and a portable stove. They watch over their kettles, buffalo milk and sugar and keep the tea (which is boiled with the milk and sugar) at the correct strength and temperature by adding more hot water, then more milk or sugar as needed, constantly adjusting the proportions. The *chai* is served in 'disposable' low-fired clay cups called *kullarhs*. These are made by hand out of native clay in open fires. Customers sip the hot, milky, sweet tea and then throw away the empty cups. Tasty fried snacks such as samosas and *bhel poori* are often

An Indian tea propaganda van.

A *chai wallah* in Calcutta serving his tea.

served with the tea. This 'railway tea' is the most common tea in India. *Masala chai* has spices added and this is particularly popular in the Punjab, Haryana and elsewhere in northern and central India; in eastern India (West Bengal and Assam) tea is generally drunk without spices.

# Irani Cafes

At the end of the nineteenth century and the early twentieth century Zoroastrian immigrants came to Bombay from Iran in search of a better livelihood. (Bombay was also home to another Zoroastrian community, the Parsis, who had come to India from Iran from the eighth century onwards.) Known as Iranis, they were quick to recognize a good business opportunity in providing workers of the city with tea and a variety of snacks from small stalls on street corners. Later they moved into shops which became known as 'Irani' cafes or restaurants. They are furnished with marble-topped tables and bent teakwood chairs; the walls are typically adorned with portraits of Zoroaster and full-length mirrors.[4] On the walls, or over the sink where you wash your hands at the back, might be an officious notice or set of instructions. Nissim Ezekiel's poem 'Irani Restaurant Instructions' sums up the brisk, yet welcoming essence of the Irani cafe:

Please
Do not spit
Do not sit more
Pay promptly, time is invaluable
Do not write letter
Without order refreshment
Do not comb
Hair is spoiling floor
Do not make mischiefs in cabin
Our waiter is reporting
Come again
All are welcome whatever caste
If not satisfied tell us

Otherwise tell others
god is great[5]

Irani cafes became well known for their strong milky sweet tea called *paani kum chai*. *Paani kum* means boiled in milk. At first the Iranis made their accustomed weak tea but the Indians, who preferred strong milky sweet tea, always asked for tea made with less water. So *paani kum chai* was born out of the needs of the customer.[6] Also served are bread buns split and spread with butter called *brun maska*, which are so crusty they are dunked into the tea. Coffee, cakes and salted biscuits were also on the menu as well as Parsi specialties such as *akoori* (spicy scrambled eggs). These cafes became well known in Bombay and later in Hyderabad. Sadly from an estimated 350 cafes in the 1950s barely 25 have survived today.

Tea is also consumed in the home. Although tea was slow to be accepted in south India, and took second place to coffee for a long time, tea is often served with tiffin, especially in Andhra Pradesh and Tamil Nadu. It is customary to be offered a 'tiffin' as a courtesy when you visit a Tamil resident. 'No day is complete without tiffin, an afternoon snack, to fill the gap between lunch and dinner. There are mobile carts, coffee shops, sweetshops and cafes on every street in Madras, selling sweets and savouries with coffee and tea.'[7]

The tradition of afternoon tea continues in West Bengal. Middle- and upper-class Bengalis drink tea accompanied by Western-style cakes and Indian savoury snacks.

# Teas of India

India has three distinct tea-growing regions that produce teas that differ in style, taste and flavour.

Assam is the largest black tea-producing region of the world. Its climate (with heavy rainfall and hot temperatures) and geography are well suited for producing rich, full-bodied teas which are ideal for blending and are recommended to be drunk with milk and sugar.

The tea leaves plucked from March until May are known as first flush and when brewed the tea has a strong and fresh aroma. In June the plucking of the second flush starts and goes through to September. This second flush produces the famous 'tippy teas', with a rich aroma, a strong malty taste and a clear dark red liquor. Assam tea picked from October to December is known as the Winter Harvest.

Tea pickers in Assam.

The cool and moist climate, the soil and sloping terrain of Darjeeling – a hill resort in the Himalayan foothills of northeast India, 1,800 m (6,000 feet) above sea level – all combine to produce teas famed for their delicate flavour, likened to Muscatel. They are often called the 'champagne of teas'.

Because of the climate and high elevation Darjeeling tea bushes do not go on growing throughout the year. The first flush is picked in April. These first teas of the season are considered the finest and are much in demand, fetching very high prices at auction. The second flush is picked between May and June and also produces excellent quality teas. Some people consider them better than the first flush as they are less astringent and fruitier. Teas picked during the monsoon

Darjeeling in the foothills of the Himalayas.

season (July to September) contain a lot of moisture and tend to have a darker colour and a strong, bitter flavour. They are generally used in breakfast blends. The autumnal flush is harvested in October and November. These teas are more robust and full-bodied than first- and second-flush teas but still much lighter than the monsoon teas..

Nilgiri teas come from the Nilgiri mountains (sometimes called the Blue Mountains) that stretch across the states of Tamil Nadu, Karnataka and Kerala in South India. Tea here is grown by 20,000 or so small holders at elevations ranging from 1,000 to 2,500 metres (3,300 to 8,000 feet). The rainfall, the geography and climate produces a tea which is fragrant but as the same time full-bodied and brisk. Nilgiri teas are often used for blending.

Tea pickers on the Glenburn Estate, Darjeeling. Glenburn is a heavenly little plantation retreat that lies on a hillock above the banks of the River Rungeet, high in the Himalayas, overlooked by the mighty Kanchenjunga mountain range.

Other areas producing tea in India are the Dooars, the floodplains and foothills of the eastern Himalayas; Sikkim, a tiny province to the west of Assam; Terai, just south of Darjeeling; the Kangra Valley in Himachal Pradesh; and Travancore, which produces teas with similar characteristics to those of Sri Lanka. A small amount of green tea is produced in the Kangra Valley, mainly for the Afghan market.

## Sri Lanka (formerly Ceylon)

Coffee was the main crop on the island of Sri Lanka until, in 1869, a coffee-rust fungus called *Hemileia vastatrix* attacked the coffee plants and devastated the coffee industry. James Taylor, an adventurous Scotsman who had come to the island in 1852 to grow coffee, was selected by the owners of Loolecondera Estate to experiment in planting some tea seeds on 19 acres of land in 1867. His pioneering spirit and perseverance

Tea pickers in Ceylon in the 1890s.

A replica of an antique Lipton's tea tin manufactured by Lipton in honour of its history.

led the way for the development of tea-growing on the island, whose climate and soil conditions proved ideal. He laid out the first of many later tea gardens, developed machinery to process the leaves, built factories and achieved excellent quality teas. He was largely responsible for the success of the country's tea business.

Rapid expansion of the tea industry in the 1870s and '80s brought a good deal of interest from large British companies, which took over many of the small estates. One man, a grocer, bought four estates. The son of poor Irish immigrants, Thomas Lipton grew up in the slums of Glasgow. At the age of ten he sailed to America, where he learned all about trade, advertising and salesmanship by working in a successful New York grocery store. He returned to Glasgow and by the age of 21 opened his own store selling groceries including tea. He was very successful and by 1890 he was a millionaire. He travelled to Ceylon to explore the possibilities of growing tea and exporting it direct to Britain. Most working-class families could not easily afford the high price of tea and Lipton's plan to reduce costs was to cut out the middleman. Lipton was also the first to sell tea exclusively in brightly coloured packages bearing the clever slogan 'direct from the tea garden to the pot'. They were sold in three qualities, the top one in a yellow packet with a red Lipton shield, which to this day typifies the Lipton Yellow Label brand. This familiar package can be seen on grocers' shelves in more than 150 countries around the world.

These teas, known as Ceylon teas, are generally classified according to the altitude at which they are grown. At each level a tea is produced which has its own unique character. High-grown tea (between 1,200 and 2,500 m, or 4,000 and 8,000 feet) produces a bright, golden, fragrant liquor; middle-grown (between 600 and 1,200 m, or 2,000 and 4,000 feet) a rich and smooth tea; and low-grown (at about 600 m or 2,000 feet) dark, strong teas.

The main tea growing areas in Sri Lanka are Galle, to the south of the island; Rathapura, east of the capital, Colombo; Kandy, a low region near the ancient royal capital; Nuwara Eliya, a high-growing area producing some very fine teas; Dimbula, grown west of the central mountains; and Uva, east of Dimbula. The teas are often blended from different areas of the island and offer a wide range of flavour and colour. They are known generally as Ceylon blend.

# Indonesia

In the early seventeenth century the Dutch East India Company (voc) was trading in Chinese commodities, including tea, with Java. They also established the first tea plantations there in the early eighteenth century. At first seeds from China were grown but these did not flourish, and so Assam bushes from India were cultivated. Later tea-growing was introduced to Sumatra. More recently production has started on the island of Sulawesi.

Tea from Indonesia, India and Ceylon dominated the world's tea markets until the Second World War. The war resulted in the destruction of the Indonesian tea estates and factories and many tea plants returned to their wild state. In 1984 a rehabilitation programme was started and the Tea Board of Indonesia was established. The industry was restructured, plantations replanted with superior cloned tea plants and factories were refurbished with new machinery. In the past Indonesia produced only black teas but due to demand and the acknowledged health benefits, green tea production was introduced in 1988.

Indonesian teas are light and fragrant with a bright liquor. Most are blended and sold as loose packaged teas or used in making tea bags. There are some Indonesian speciality teas, such as Gunung Rosa, Talon and Bah Buton. These teas are best enjoyed without milk, perhaps with some lemon.

The Indonesian word for tea is *tey* and the drinking customs vary according to the region. Some Indonesians drink tea without any sugar. In Java, however, they do, perhaps because the sugar plantations are located in that region, not just to sweeten what is called *tey pahit* or *tey tawar*, meaning 'bitter tea'. Western Java restaurants commonly serve plain tea as a substitute for water, partly for health and safety reasons, since the water has been boiled to make the tea.

Indonesians are great 'snackers' and tea-drinkers. Street vendors serve glasses of sweet, perfumed tea to office workers. Tea is often served after the midday meal and then again at 'afternoon tea', when it is served with rice cakes, fried bananas and so on at about half past four.[8]

# 7
# Tea Today and Tomorrow

From its early history in the East, tea has become one of the world's ubiquitous drinks. Tea-drinking in one form or another is part of the diverse cultures of many lands, and chameleon-like, tea has absorbed national influences and taken on different styles and uses far distant from the Oriental original. While 'true' tea derives from the leaf of a camellia plant, what an amazing diversity of beverages that same leaf can produce! The strong, robust brew of a British soldier taking a break somewhere hot and dangerous might seem very far removed from the refined devotees at a Japanese tea ceremony. The faint aroma of jasmine gathered at the rim of a delicate Chinese porcelain cup is very different from the rich and heavily spiced *masala chai* served to passengers in clay cups at busy railway stations in India. Yet tea is what every one of these very different people drink; tea from the generous plant with the magic leaves.

William Gladstone, a Prime Minister during Queen Victoria's reign, is recorded to have said of tea:

> If you are cold, tea will warm you; if you are heated, it will cool you; if you're depressed, it will cheer you; if you're excited, it will calm you.

Recent years have seen considerable interest in tea's therapeutic properties, which is one of the factors leading to an increase in tea consumption. We have come full circle from tea's early origins in China and its arrival in Europe, when it was esteemed for its ability to dispel tiredness, to stimulate the mind and to raise energy levels, even help banish fevers and cure head and stomach problems. Modern scientific research in both East and West has found that regular tea-drinking can lower blood fats and prevent cholesterol accumulation. Tea-drinking is also said to help with weight loss, prevent tooth decay and gum disease and helps stimulate the kidneys and other internal organs. Some studies suggest it protects against certain cancers, as the antioxidants in tea 'soak up' free radicals. The health benefits of tea are the basis for continuing research.

The future of tea as a beverage looks sound and its continued popularity around the world seems assured. In the

A poster put out by the Empire Tea Market Expansion Bureau in Britain in the 1930s.

United Kingdom alone it is estimated that 165 million cups of tea are consumed daily. At the same time, new trends are emerging: tea-drinkers are demanding tea which is cultivated sustainably and organically, sourced ethically and traded fairly. Flavoured teas have also become popular.

Whether hot or cold, strong or weak, black or green, sweet or smoky, oolong or pekoe, with milk or lemon, bag or leaf, tea is the universal drink of countless millions.

A brief history of tea's origins and how it is made and used can only give a general impression of its worldwide significance. This book attempts to do that in the hope that interested readers may be stimulated to delve further themselves into the fascinating story that began when the first cup of tea was infused in China many long years ago.

# Recipes

## What gives tea its flavour and aroma?

The chemistry of tea is extremely complex. Its flavour comes from a combination of three main components: caffeine, catechins and theanine. Caffeine imparts bitterness to the taste and also acts as a mild stimulant. All types of tea contain caffeine but in different quantities; the amount also depends on the strength of the tea brewed. Catechins are part of a class of chemical compounds called polyphenols (often referred to as tannins) and they provide the tea's 'briskness' or astringency. If tea is overbrewed they can give off a bitter taste. Theanine is an amino acid which adds sweetness to the flavour and helps suppress the stimulant function of caffeine.

The aroma of teas can be strikingly varied in different teas depending on how the tea is produced. Japanese green teas which are steamed have grassy, seaweed notes while Chinese green teas which are pan-fried and dried produce savoury, toasted notes. Enzyme activity in semi-fermented oolong and fermented black teas liberates floral, fruity and much richer, stronger aromas.

Tea can be used as a flavouring for a variety of dishes: marinades and cooking liquids; in creams, sorbets, ices, creams and ice cream; in jellies; and in cakes, biscuits and scones.

There are many different ways of preparing tea as a beverage depending on the type and quality of the tea, the region, the occasion and individual tastes. Some teas are better infused for a short time, others for longer. The quality and temperature of the water is also a consideration: tea connoisseurs often use spring water to make the tea and a thermometer to ensure the right water temperature. For most brews it is essential that as soon as the water boils it should be poured over the tea leaves.

A mid-nineteenth recipe or guidance for making tea in the United Kingdom was given by Mrs Beeton in her book *Beeton's Book of Household Management* (London, 1861).

## To Make Tea

There is very little art in making good tea; if the water is boiling, and there is no sparing of the fragrant leaf, the beverage will almost invariably be good. The old-fashioned plan of allowing a teaspoonful to each person, and one over, is still practised. Warm the teapot with *boiling* water; let it remain for two or three minutes for the vessel to become thoroughly hot, then pour it away. Put in the tea, pour in from ½ to ¾ pint of *boiling* water, close the lid, and let it stand for the tea to draw from 5 to 10 minutes; then fill up the pot with water. The tea will be quite spoiled unless made with water that is actually boiling, as the leaves will not open, and the flavour not be extracted from them; the beverage will consequently be colourless and tasteless – in fact, nothing but tepid water.

## Moroccan Tea

1 ½ tablespoons green tea
4 cups (1 litre) boiling water
4–5 oz (100–150 g) sugar lumps
a handful of fresh mint

Add the tea leaves to a pot and pour a little boiling water over them. Swirl it round and carefully pour this water away. Add the sugar and the fresh mint. Pour in the remaining boiling water, push down the mint into the liquid and infuse for 2–3 minutes. Serve in traditional tea glasses or tea cups.

# Iced Tea

This recipe has been given to me by Jane Davidson, the American wife of the late Alan Davidson.

1 tall glass about 6 inches/15 cm
an iced teaspoon or a long handled teaspoon
a teapot (not metal)
a Pyrex jug
2 teaspoons loose tea (Liptons in the US;
English Breakfast in the UK)
lemon
fresh mint
granulated sugar
ice cubes

Bring 1¼ cup (275 ml) of water to the boil. Add the tea into the teapot. Pour the boiling water over the tea leaves. Let stand for 5 minutes or so. Strain into a Pyrex jug or vessel and allow to cool. Put into the refrigerator until required.

Pour the cold tea over ice cubes which have been placed in the tall glass. Cut a slice of lemon, split this halfway through and install it on side of glass. Rinse a stalk of mint and place it in beside the lemon.

Put the glass on a saucer (when the spoon has been used, it will need a place on which it can drip).

To serve, pass the granulated sugar so your guest can add the desired amount. The lemon garnish and mint can now be added to the tea. Give a good stir, and squash the lemon and mint with the spoon. Enjoy the sound effects of tinkling ice. What bliss on a hot summer's day.

# Tea Cups and Punches

The tradition of drinking punches and cups was brought to Britain from India. The name punch is thought to derive from the Persian *panj* or Hindi *panch* meaning 'five', from the five ingredients: sugar, spirits, lemon or lime juice, water and spices. Some later variations included tea. Punch also became very popular in North America.

## Eliza Acton's The Regent's, or George The Fourth's, Punch

Pare as thin as possible the rinds of two China oranges, of two lemons, and of one Seville orange, and infuse them for an hour in half a pint of thin cold syrup; then add to them the juice of the fruit. Make a pint of strong green tea, sweeten it well with fine sugar, and when it is quite cold, add it to the fruit and syrup, with a glass of the best old Jamaica rum, a glass of brandy, one of arrack, one of pine-apple syrup, and two bottles of champagne; pass the whole through a fine lawn sieve until it is perfectly clear, then bottle, and put it into ice until dinner is served. We are indebted for this receipt to a person who made the punch daily for the prince's table, at Carlton palace, for six months, it has been in our possession some years, and may be relied upon.

## Tea Cup

This tea cup has been adapted from Mrs Leyel's recipe in *The Gentle Art of Cookery* (1929).

3 cups (700 ml) strong Indian tea
1 cup (225 ml) green tea
3 cups (700 ml) sparkling mineral water
rind of 1 lemon
1 oz (25 g) sugar

4 borage leaves (or substitute mint)
ice cubes
½ cup (110 ml) curaçao

Make the two types of tea and then mix them together in a large bowl. Add the mineral water, the lemon rind, sugar and borage leaves. Add some ice cubes and the curaçao and give a good stir.

Place the bowl on ice to keep chilled and serve.

## Spiced Tea

This has been adapted from Rabbi Blue's 'Matchmaker's Tea' in his book *Kitchen Blues* (1985).

Make a pot of black Indian tea for two to four people. Into each cup put a 1 inch (2.5 cm) cinnamon stick, a slice of lemon, 1 tablespoon lemon juice, 2 teaspoons sugar and 3 tablespoons rum and pour over the hot tea.

For a cooling drink in summer add ice cubes before pouring the tea over.

# Tea as a flavouring

## Chinese Tea Eggs

12 eggs
1 teaspoon salt
3 tablespoons light or dark soy sauce
2 star anise
1 teaspoon five-spice powder
3 tablespoons black China tea leaves

Hard-boil the eggs for six to eight minutes. Drain and roll the eggs gently on a hard surface until the shell cracks finely all over but do not peel.

Put the eggs back in the saucepan, cover with fresh water, add the salt, soy sauce, spices and tea leaves. Bring to the boil and simmer for about one hour. Allow the eggs to cool in the liquid.

Shell the eggs to reveal a beautiful marbled pattern and serve.

## Shrimps in Dragon Well Tea

The dish is usually made with freshwater shrimps but shrimps or prawns from the sea can be substituted.

12 oz (350 g) peeled uncooked prawns or shrimps
1 teaspoon salt
1 egg white
1 tablespoon cornstarch
1 tablespoon Dragon Well Tea
½ cup (110 ml) boiling water
4 teaspoons groundnut oil
1 tablespoon rice wine or dry sherry
1 spring onion (scallion) finely chopped

Devein the shrimps if necessary. Rinse well under cold running water and then pat dry with paper towels. Rub the shrimp evenly with salt, mix in the egg white and cornstarch and set aside to marinate for about 15 minutes.

Put the tea leaves in a bowl or measuring cup. Bring the water to a boil and pour over the tea leaves. Let the tea steep for 15 minutes then drain, reserving both the liquid and the tea leaves.

Heat a wok or large frying pan until it is hot and add the oil. Add the shrimp mixture and stir-fry for 30 seconds. Add half of the reserved tea leaves and the reserved tea water and cook for another minute adding the wine and the spring onions. Mix thoroughly, then serve.

## O-chazuke

*O-chazuke* is a simple Japanese tea-flavoured rice dish. The word comes from *o-cha* meaning tea and *tzuke* meaning to submerge. The rice is topped with a variety of other ingredients such as fragments of salmon, shreds of nori (seaweed), pieces of *umeboshi* (pickles), wasabi and toasted sesame seeds (all of which can come dried out of packets), and then the hot tea is poured over it. *O-chazuke* is a favourite midnight snack and is also eaten after an evening's drinking as a hangover cure. Any kind of green tea can be used but many people prefer *hoji-cha* or *genmai-cha*.

4 cups hot cooked rice
6 tablespoons flaked cooked salmon
6 tablespoons shredded toasted nori seaweed
a little umeboshi (dried, salt-pickled Japanese apricot)
some pickled daikon (white mooli/radish)
2 finely chopped green onions
some toasted sesame seeds
2 teaspoons wasabi
6 cups hot green tea

Place the hot rice into a large bowl, or four individual serving bowls. Add the toppings according to taste. Pour over the hot tea to cover the rice and leave to infuse for about a minute or so to allow the flavours to develop.

## Lemon and Rose Tea Jelly

Tea jellies can be made with gelatine or, as in this recipe, with pectin or jam sugar. They are delicious served as a dessert with cream, ice-cream or yoghurt or for breakfast served on toast like jam or marmalade. Any kind of tea can be used but preferably a scented one.

2 lemons
220 ml (1 cup) of water, plus 425 ml (2 cups) water

for brewing the tea
2 tablespoons rose scented tea
600 gm (3 cups) jam sugar

Grate or zest the peel of the lemons and then squeeze out the juice. Add the lemon juice and zest to a cup of water. Set to one side. Bring the 2 cups of water to the boil and pour over the tea. Allow to infuse for about five minutes, then strain the tea into a preserving pan or suitable saucepan and discard the tea leaves. Bring the tea liquid to a boil and add the lemon juice, zest and jam sugar. Stir and bring back to the boil and continue cooking for about four minutes. This should make a soft jelly, not a thick-set jam.

Spoon the jelly into sterilized jars, cover with waxed paper circles and allow to cool and set.

## Green Tea Ice Cream

This recipe has been adapted from Setsuko Yoshizuka's recipe at http://japanesefood.about.com. It is made from Japanese *matcha*, which gives the ice-cream a vibrant colour.

1 level tablespoon *matcha* green tea powder
3 tablespoons hot water
2 egg yolks
5 tablespoons sugar
¾ cup (175 ml) milk
¾ cup (175 ml) double cream

Mix the green tea powder with the hot water together in a bowl and set aside. Lightly whisk the eggs yolks in a pan and then add the sugar and mix well. Gradually add the milk to the egg and sugar mixture, mixing well. Place the pan over a low heat and heat the mixture, stirring constantly.

When the mixture thickens, remove the pan from the heat. Cool by placing the bottom of the pan in a bowl of ice cold water.

Leaving the bottom of the pan in the ice water, add the green tea liquid to the egg mixture and stir well. Whip the cream and stir into the mixture, folding in gently.

Pour the whole mixture into an ice cream maker and freeze, following the instructions of the ice cream maker. Alternatively, pour the mixture into a container and freeze in a freezer which has been turned to its coldest setting, removing from the freezer once or twice to whisk up the ice cream and prevent large ice crystals from forming.

## Jasmine Tea Sorbet

2 cups (425 ml) water plus 2½ cups (570 ml) water
7 oz (200 g) caster sugar, plus 4 oz (110 g)
Rind and juice of 1 lemon
4 teaspoons jasmine tea
2 egg whites
mint leaves and lemon slices for the garnish

Make a syrup by mixing 425 ml of water with 200 g caster sugar in a pan with the lemon rind and bring to a boil. Turn down the heat and leave to bubble slowly for about ten minutes then remove from the heat and add the lemon juice. Pour into a container and allow to cool.

Place the tea leaves in a bowl and pour over 570 ml boiling water. Allow to infuse for about 10 minutes, then strain and leave to cool. Blend with the syrup. Place in a container and put in the freezer. Remove it when half frozen and prepare a meringue with the 2 egg whites and remaining 110 g caster sugar. Whisk the egg whites until very stiff. Fold in the caster sugar. Whisk the half frozen tea mixture until mushy then slowly fold into the meringue mixture. Return to the freezer and refreeze.

Remove the sorbet from the freezer about half an hour before serving so that the texture is fairly soft and mushy. Whisk or stir it up with a fork if necessary. Garnish with the mint and lemon.

# Tea Loaf

Tea loaf is often served with afternoon tea. Use Yorkshire Tea for a strong flavour or Lady Grey for a more delicate taste. Serve thinly sliced, spread with a little butter.

2 teaspoons loose tea
4½ oz (125 g) Demerara sugar
11 oz (300 g) green and red raisins mixed
grated rind and juice of ½ orange
8 oz (225 g) self-raising flour
1 tsp cinnamon
2 medium eggs, beaten

Place the tea into a heat-proof jug or bowl and add 1½ cups (300 ml) boiling water. Allow to infuse for 5 minutes. Strain the tea and discard the tea leaves. Stir in the sugar and allow to dissolve.

Pour the tea over the raisins in another bowl and add the orange rind and juice. Mix well then leave in a cool place for at least 4 hours, but preferably overnight.

Line a 1 kg loaf tin with baking parchment and preheat the oven to 180°C (350°F), or gas mark 4.

Sift the flour with the cinnamon over the raisins and their liquid. Stir in the eggs and beat the mixture well. Pour into the loaf tin and bake in the oven for about 1–1½ hours or until a skewer comes out clean.

Allow the loaf to cool in the tin for about 10 minutes.

# Tea Cup Trifle

This trifle is made in tea cups. Use glass or delicate decorative porcelain cups for the best effect.

1 heaped tablespoon rose scented tea
sugar to taste
8 boudoir biscuits
a little strawberry jam
1 ⅓ cups (300 ml) rich thick custard
1 cup (250 ml) whipping cream
1 teaspoon rose water
1 teaspoon icing sugar
crystallized rose petals and violets to decorate

First of all make the tea by pouring ½ cup (120 ml) boiling water over the tea leaves in a measuring jug and leave to infuse for 15 to 20 minutes. Sweeten to taste. Smear the boudoir biscuits with strawberry jam, break each one into three or four pieces and divide equally into four cups. Strain the tea and gently pour the tea liquid in equal quantities over the boudoir biscuits. Spoon the custard evenly over the top of the biscuits. Add the rose water and the icing sugar to the cream and whip until stiff. Swirl on top of the custard. Decorate with the crystallized rose petals and violets.

# Glossary

Below are some of the main types of teas and tea blends.

**Afternoon tea:** a blend of delicate Darjeeling with high grown Ceylon tea.

**Assam:** a full-bodied black tea from north-east India.

**Bancha:** the everyday tea of Japan.

**Bohea:** a term rarely used today, but originally one of the most sought-after black China teas from the Wuyi Shan mountains.

**Caravan teas:** sometimes called China Caravan or Russian Caravan because they originally came overland to Russia by the camel caravan routes from China.

**Ceylon:** a general name for black teas produced in Sri Lanka.

**Chai:** a black tea with a blend of spices, giving a rich and spicy flavour. It is popular in the USA and in India where it is usually known as *masala chai*.

**Chrysanthemum tea:** is not a real tea. It consists of the dried pale yellow blossoms infused like tea.

**Chun Mee:** a green tea from China, also known as 'precious eyebrow'. It is the shape of the processed leaves which give this tea its name, as they resemble the finely shaped eyebrows of a young girl. The tea has a clear yellow liquor and a smooth taste.

**Congou:** a fine quality Chinese black tea with a large leaf. It is obtained from the fifth and largest leaf gathered from a shoot tip of the tea plant. It is commonly layered with rose petals or buds, which lend a delightful flowery scent to the tea; it is then called rose congou. The name comes from the Chinese word *gongfu*, and as a tea-brewing term, it means 'art of tea brewing'.

**Darjeeling:** a delicate black tea from India.

**Dimbula:** probably the most famous of Ceylon black teas, noted for its body and aroma.

**Dragon Well tea:** see Long Jing.

**Earl Grey:** a blend of China black teas scented with oil of bergamot, which is made from the peel of *Citrus bergamia*. It is named after a nineteenth-century British statesman, the second Earl Grey, who was given the recipe during a diplomatic mission to China. It is best drunk without milk or sugar.

**English Breakfast:** usually a blend of Indian and Ceylon black teas which has a strong, full-bodied brisk flavour. An ideal breakfast drink, it is usually drunk with milk, and often sugar.

**Genmaicha:** a kind of **bancha** (see above).

**Gongfu:** means leisure or meditative breathing and the Chinese characters convey the meaning of requiring skill and patience to brew this tea. The brewing of *gongfu* tea is an art which can possibly be traced back to the monks of the Song monasteries and is now a speciality of the region of Fujian and Taiwan.

The tea is made with oolong tea in a small Yixing teapot and served in very small cups. See also **congou**.

**Gunpowder:** a green tea whose leaves are rolled into small round pellets. When the British first arrived in China and were shown the tea they called it gunpowder on account of its resemblance to the gunpowder pellets used for cannons. The Chinese themselves call it pearl tea. If only the tenderest buds and tips are used it is generally known as Pinhead Gunpowder. Gunpowder has a straw-coloured liquor with a mild and delicate taste. See also **Imperial**.

**Gyokuro:** the finest and most expensive of Japanese teas.

**H. M. Blend:** a blend of several teas which was made especially for Queen Victoria.

**Hyson:** is a grade description of a China green tea. The tea is processed as long, thin twisted leaves. The best of this tea, which is picked in early spring, is called Young Hyson.

**Imperial:** is a grade description of the loosely balled older and larger leaf which is sifted out of Gunpowder tea proper.

**Irish Breakfast:** is usually a blend of rich, malty Assam teas although sometimes African and Indonesian teas are added.

**Keemun:** is one of the most sought-after black teas and is renowned for its pale, gold liquor, fruity but subtle aroma and delicate taste. It comes from Andhui Province in China. In England it is popular with breakfast and is one of the prominent ingredients of the English Breakfast blend.

**Kenilworth:** a black tea from Sri Lanka which has long, wiry but beautiful leaves, producing an almost oaky taste.

**Kenya:** a black tea from Kenya which has a deep reddish gold liquor.

**Kombucha:** a type of health drink tea made by fermenting tea and sugar with kombucha culture, which turns the sweet tea into a drink full of vitamins, minerals, enzymes and health-giving organic acids. The tea tastes a little like sparkling cider. Kombucha probably originated in the Far East.

**Lady Grey:** is a delicate and fragrant variation of the more famous Earl Grey tea. It is blend of black teas, scented with orange, lemon, bergamot and cornflowers.

**Lady Londonderry:** a tea named after a society hostess in the early part of the twentieth century. She had her own blend of Ceylon, Indian and Formosa tea made for her by Jacksons of Piccadilly.

**Lapsang souchong:** a speciality black tea from Fujian province in China with a distinct smoky aroma and flavour and a rich red liquor. See also **souchong** below.

**Lay Jee:** (Lychee), a black or oolong tea scented with yellow lychee blossoms, chiefly from Taiwan.

**Long Jing:** one of the most famous green teas of China.

**Mao Shan:** a green tea grown around the base of the Taoist mountain Mao Shan. Emperors of the Tang and Song dynasties were served this tea, which was made with the dew collected from the needles of the pine trees growing on the slopes.

**Matcha:** a powdered green tea of Japan.

**Maté:** see **Paraguay Tea**.

**Nilgiri:** black teas from the Nilgiri mountains in India.

**Nuwara Eliya:** black teas from Sri Lanka which are light, delicate with a fragrant flavour.

**Paraguay Tea:** or Jesuit's Tea, also known as maté, is not a tea at all. It is a drink made from the dried leaves of the yerba, *Ilex paraguariensis*, which is indigenous to Paraguay and other parts of Latin America. It can be drunk like ordinary tea. It has quite a bitter taste and is not usually sweetened.

**Pouchong:** a very lightly fermented tea, something between a green tea and oolong. It originated in Fujian, China, and was taken to Taiwan. The name means 'the wrapped kind', because during fermentation the leaves were originally wrapped in five-ounce packs in paper made from cotton. Pouchong has a smooth flavour and sweet taste with an amber-coloured liquor. It is now made mostly in Taiwan from the long, thin Fujian-type leaf and is often used as a base for scented teas such as jasmine or rose pouchong.

**Rooibos:** (pronounced 'roy-boss') is a 'red tea' produced in South Africa which has become very popular in the West as a healthy alternative to tea. It is caffeine-free and rich in antioxidants. It is made from the shrub *Aspalathus linearis*, which grows only in a small area in the Cederberg region of the Western Cape province of South Africa. The word rooibos means 'red bush' in Afrikaans. The green, needle-like leaves of the plant turn a deep red colour when cut and left to dry in the sun.

**Russian:** a black tea from Georgia. See **caravan tea** above.

**Saint James:** a coppery-coloured black tea from Sri Lanka with a smooth taste.

**Sencha:** a green tea from Japan.

**Souchong:** is a high-grade variety of black tea originally from Fujian province in China. In Cantonese *siu chung* means 'small sort' and is a reference to the fine leaves. Lapsang souchong is the smoky version of souchong.

**Tung Ting:** a special oolong tea considered the best tea grown in Taiwan's premier oolong-growing region, Nantou country. It is a tea for special occasions. It is often referred to as one of the 'Orchid oolongs' or, because of its golden green liquor, 'jade', and has a gentle, smooth and soft taste.

**Twankey:** often refers to an unrolled tea leaf of a poor quality but it is really the name given to a size of leaf of green tea. The name twankey has been immortalized by 'Widow Twankey' in the pantomime version of Aladdin.

**Welsh Brew:** a strong tea blended from quality African and Indian black teas (mainly in the form of tea bags) made by Murroughs in Wales.

**Yorkshire Tea:** England's best-selling top-quality tea; over 10 million cups of Yorkshire tea are drunk every day. Made by Taylors of Harrogate, many people believe it is tea grown on Ilkley Moor in Yorkshire, but it is in fact a blend of top-quality Assam and African teas. There are four blends including the original blend and Gold, a luxury blend with lots of strength, character and flavour.

**Yunnan:** a black tea from China produced from a strain of ancient native Yunnan Dayeh (broad-leafed) tea tree which is also used for Puerh teas. It has a sweet delicate aroma and a clear liquor.

**Zulu tea:** a name given to a tea which Taylors of Harrogate discovered on the Ntingwe Tea estate deep in the wooded hills of Kwazulu Natal in the 1990s and which they now market. It has a fresh, brisk flavour and a bright liquor. They also use it in their Yorkshire Tea blend.

# References

## Introduction

1 Mt Penglai was the traditional home of the immortals. From 'Seven Bowls of Tea' by Lu Tong, a poet of the Tang Dynasty, trans. from Kit Chow and Ione Kramer, *All the Tea in China* (San Francisco, CA, 1990).

## 1 What is Tea?

1 Robert Fortune, *A Journey to the Tea Countries of China* (London, 1852) p. 237.

## 2 China

1 William H. Ukers, *The Romance of Tea* (New York, 1936), p. 7.
2 Ibid., p. 8.
3 Lu Yü, *The Classic of Tea*, trans. and introduced by Francis Ross Carpenter (Boston, 1974), pp. 70–72, 105–7, 107.
4 Trans. in John Blofeld, *The Chinese Art of Tea* (Boston, 1985), p. 136.
5 Carole Manchester, *Tea in the East* (New York, 1996), p. 12.
6 Fuchsia Dunlop, *Sichuan Cookery* (London, 2003), p. 239.

7  Yan-Kit So, *Classic Food of China* (London, 1992), p. 71.
8  Ibid., p. 72.


## 3 Japan, Korea and Taiwan

1  Richard Hosking, *At the Japanese Table* (New York, 2000), p. 29.
2  Naomichi Ishige, *The History and Culture of Japanese Food* (London, 2001), p. 87.
3  Michael J. Pettid, *Korean Cuisine* (London, 2008), pp. 124–7.


## 4 Caravans and Mediterranean Shores

1  Rinjing Dorje, *Food in Tibetan Life* (London, 1985), p. 53.
2  Daw Aung San Suu Kyi, '"Taking Tea", Gathering at the TeaShops', 14 April 1996, at www.dassk.com, last accessed 21 December 2009.
3  Lady Macartney, *An English Lady in Chinese Turkestan* (repr. Oxford, 1985), pp. 66–7.
4  George Abraham Grierson, *A Dictionary of the Kashmiri Language* (Calcutta, 1932).
5  Roland and Sabrina Michaud, *Caravans to Tartary* (London, 1978).
6  Saleb or salep is a milky drink thickened with salep, a starchy powder made by drying and pulverizing the root tubers of certain plants of the orchid family.
7  O. S. Gökyay, ed., *Evliya Celebi Seyyahatnamesi*, Book 1 (Istanbul, 1996), vol. 1, p. 261.


## 5 Tea Comes to the West

1  As quoted in Reay Tannahill, *Food in History* (London, 1988), p. 267. Rhubarb was a Chinese plant much prized by European apothecaries for medicinal purposes.
2  Jan Huyghen van Linschoten, *The Voyage to the East Indies*,

vol. 1 (London, 1885), p. 157.

3  N. Hudson Moore, *Delftware: Dutch and English* (New York, 1908), p. 16.

4  At www.easterntea.com, last accessed 22 December 2009.

5  Carole Manchester, *French Tea* (New York, 1993), p. 17.

6  At www.mariagefreres.com, last accessed 22 December 2009.

7  Bee Wilson, *Swindled* (London, 2008), pp. 31–3.

8  Wolfgang Schivelbush, *Tastes of Paradise* (New York, 1993) pp 79–84.

9  Edward Bramah, *Tea and Coffee* (London, 1972), p. 50.

10  From William Cowper's *The Task* (1784) and later used as a slogan promoting tea as an alternative to alcohol in the mid-nineteenth century associated with the Temperance Movement.

11  Beatrice Crozier, *The Tango and How to Dance It* (1913), quoted from Susan Cohen, *Where to Take Tea* (London, 2003), p. 28.

12  'The Boston Tea Party, 1773', at www.eyewitnesstohistory.com/teaparty.htm, last accessed 22 December 2009.

13  The title is Australian slang for travelling on foot with one's belongings in a 'Matilda' (bag) slung over one's back.

## 6 India, Sri Lanka and Indonesia

1  *The Voyages and Travels of J. Albert de Mandelslo . . .* (1669), p. 13.

2  Carole Manchester, *Tea in the East* (New York, 1996), p. 104.

3  Jennifer Brennan, *Curries and Bugles* (London, 1992), p. 153.

4  Suketu Mehta, *Maximum City: Bombay Lost and Found* (New York, 2005), p. 261.

5  At http://parsikhabar.net/a-taste-of-persia-and-old-bombay-irani-chai, accessed 23 December 2009. My thanks to Elkana Ezekiel for permission to quote this poem.

6  Cyrus Todiwala, personal communication.

7  Rani Kingman, *Flavours of Madras* (Reading, 1994), p. 124.

8  Sri Owen, *Indonesian Food and Cookery* (London, 1986), p. 16.

# Select Bibliography

*The Book of Tea* (Paris, n.d.)
*Mariage Frères: The French Art of Tea* (Paris, 1997)
Avery, Martha, *The Tea Road* (Beijing, 2003)
Bald, C., *Indian Tea* (Calcutta, 1933)
Blofeld, John, *The Chinese Art of Tea* (Boston, MA, 1985)
Bramah, Edward, *The Bramah Tea and Coffee Walk Around London*
    (London, 2005)
—, *Tea and Coffee* (London, 1972)
Brother Anthony of Taizé and Hong Kyeong-Hee, *The Korean*
    *Way of Tea* (Seoul, 2007)
Chow, Kit, and Ione Kramer, *All the Tea in China* (San Francisco,
    CA, 1990)
Collingham, Lizzie, *Curry: A Biography* (London, 2005)
Faulkner, Rupert, ed., *Tea: East and West* (London, 2003)
Fortune, Robert, *A Journey to the Tea Countries of China* (London,
    1852)
Forrest, Denys, *Tea for the British* (London, 1973)
Gööck, Roland, *Tea* (Künzelsau, 1990)
Griffiths, John, *Tea: The Drink That Changed the World* (London,
    2007)
Gustafson, Helen, *The Agony of the Leaves* (New York, 1996)
Hardy, Serena, *The Tea Book* (Weybridge, 1979)
Heiss, Mary Lou, and Robert J. Heiss, *The Story of Tea* (Berkeley,
    CA, 2007)
Hesse, Eelco, *Tea: The Eyelids of Bodhidharma* (Dorchester, 1982)

Kinchin, Perilla, *Taking Tea with Mackintosh: The Story of Miss Cranston's Tea Rooms* (Fullbridge Maldon, 1998)

Kuzucu, Kemalettin, 'Tea as a New Flavour in the Ottoman Culinary Culture', in *Turkish Cuisine* (Ankara, 2008)

Lancaster, Osbert, *The Story of Tea*, revd edn (London, 1958)

Mair, Victor H., and Erling Hoh, *The True History of Tea* (London, 2009)

Manchester, Carole, *French Tea: The Pleasures of the Table* (New York, 1993)

—, *Tea in the East* (New York, 1996)

McCoy, Elin, and John Frederick Walker, *Coffee and Tea* (New York, 1988)

Moxham, Roy, *Tea* (London, 2004)

Norman, Jill, *Teas and Tisanes* (Toronto, 1989)

Okakura, Kakuzo, *The Book of Tea* (New York, 1964)

Pettigrew, Jane, *Afternoon Tea* (Andover, 2004)

—, *A Social History of Tea* (London, 2001)

—, *The Tea Companion* (London, 1997)

Pratt, James Norwood, *The Tea Lover's Treasury* (San Francisco, CA, 1982)

Repplier, Agnes, *To Think of Tea!* (London, 1933)

Saberi, Helen, 'Silk Kebab and Pink Tea', in *Look and Feel*, Proceedings of the Oxford Symposium on Food and Cookery 1993 (Totnes, 1994)

Sangmanee, Kitti Cha, Catherine Donzel, Stéphane Melchior-Durand and Alain Stella, *The Little Book of Tea* (Paris, 2001)

Schapira, Joel, and Karl David, *The Book of Coffee and Tea* (New York, 1975)

Smith, Michael, ed., *The Afternoon Tea Book* (New York, 1986)

Stella, Alain, ed., *Mariage Frères: French Tea* (Paris, 2003)

Twining, Sam, *My Cup of Tea* (London, 2002)

Ukers, William H., *The Romance of Tea* (New York, 1936)

Wild, Jonathan, *Hearts, Tarts and Rascals: The Story of Bettys* (Harrogate, 2005)

Woodward, Nancy Hyden, *Teas of the World* (New York, 1980)

Yates, Jill, *Tales of a Tea Leaf* (New York, 2005)

Yu, Lü, *The Classic of Tea*, intro. and trans. Francis Ross
Carpenter (Boston, MA, 1974)

# Websites and Associations

## Tea Information and History

UK Tea Council
www.tea.co.uk

Tea Association of the USA, The Tea Council of the USA and
the Specialty Tea Institute
www.teausa.org

Tea Muse Monthly Newsletter
www.teamuse.com

## Tea Suppliers

These websites also provide history and information about tea.

East Teas
www.eastteas.com

Jing Tea
www.jingtea.com

Liptons
www.lipton.com

Mariage Frères
www.mariagefreres.com

Postcard Teas
www.postcardteas.co.uk

Puerh Tea Online Resource
www.tuochatea.com

Rare Tea Company
www.rareteacompany.com

South Silk Road
www.southsilkroad.com

The Stash Tea Company
www.stashtea.com

Twinings
www.twinings.com

Future Generation: The Vietnam Tea Exporter
www.vietnam-tea.com

Bubble Tea Supply
www.bubbleteasupply.com

# Acknowledgements

This book would not have been possible without the help, advice and encouragement of many people. I would like to thank Jonathan Barnicoat of Tregothnan Teas, Jonathan Bennett, Gwen Chesnais, Jane Davidson, Tim Doffay of Postcard Teas, Fuchsia Dunlop, Shansank Goel, Hattie Ellis, Professor Richard Hosking, Gaitri Pagrach-Chandra, Charles Perry, Gillian Riley, Alex Saberi, Aylin Öney Tan, Cyrus Todiwala, Berrin Torolosan, Stephen Twining of Twinings, Mary Williamson and Raihana Zaka.

Special thanks go to Hilary Hyman, for her constant support and enthusiasm. She not only found for me many rare books about tea, but also gave me some of the tea items photographed for this book.

My heartfelt thanks and gratitude go to David Burnett and Colleen Sen who read through my drafts and gave me so many helpful suggestions, comments and advice. They have both given me constant encouragement throughout.

I am also grateful to Michael Leaman and his team at Reaktion Books for all their helpful suggestions and guidance.

# Photo Acknowledgements

The author and publishers wish to express their thanks to the below sources of illustrative material and/or permission to reproduce it. Locations of some artworks not credited in the captions are also given below.

Advertising Archives: p. 97; from George Francklin Atkinson, *'Curry and Rice' on Forty Plates: or, The Ingredients of Social Life at 'Our Station' in India*, 5th edn [1859] (London, Calcutta and Simla, 1911): p. 132; from Isabella Mary Beeton, *The Book of Household Management . . .* (London, 1892): p. 105; Behzad Bookstore, Kabul, Afghanistan: p. 72; courtesy Bettys & Taylors of Harrogate: p. 109; photo © The Board of Trustees of the Royal Botanic Gardens, Kew: p. 11; photo Brynn Bruijn/Saudi Aramco World/SAWDIA: p. 69; Fine Arts Museums of San Francisco: p. 87; from Robert Fortune, *A Journey to the Tea Countries of China. . .* (London, 1852): p. 129; photo Patrick Frilet/Rex Features: p. 25; photo Luca Gagno: p. 61; Giraudon/ The Bridgeman Art Library: p. 89; courtesy of Max Hamilton-Little: p. 105; photo Image Source/Rex Features: p. 80; photo Sergey Kahn: p. 64; Courtesy Ali Konyalı/Ameli Edgü: p. 79; photo Library of Congress, Washington, DC: p. 117; The Metropolitan Museum of Art, New York: pp. 33 (foot), 116; Musee Condé, Chantilly: p. 89; photo Nagy Miklós: p. 75; photo National Maritime Museum, London: p. 95; photo © otokimus/2010 iStock International Inc.: p. 55; photo © Pietus/2010 iStock International Inc.: p. 6; courtesy Postcard Teas, London: pp. 40, 50, 51, 81, 134, 137, 138,

139; private collection: p. 44; Ryan Pyle/ryanpyle.com: pp. 34–5; from Rinjing Dorje, *Food in Tibetan Life* (London, 1985), reproduced by permission of the author: p. 60; photo Roger-Viollet/Rex Features: p. 90; from Thomas Rowlandson, *Picturesque Beauties of Boswell . . .* (London, 1786): p. 99; photo Ryu Seunghoo: p. 52; photos Alex Saberi: pp. 32, 62, 82, 119, 122; photo Nasir Saberi: p. 66; photo Julija Sapic/Big Stock Photo: p. 78; photo Sipa Press/Rex Features: p. 37; courtesy Steven Snodgrass: p. 141; photos Ken Straiton/Rex Features: pp. 21, 33 (top), 36; photo Tea Board, India: p. 133; courtesy the artist (Robert Todonai/Todonaiart.com): p. 124; TopFoto (© Topham Picturepoint/topfoto.co.uk): p. 110; TopFoto/HIP: p. 108; courtesy Tregothnan Teas, Cornwall: p. 112; courtesy Twinings: pp. 19, 24, 99, 100–1, 103; Victoria & Albert Museum, London: pp. 17, 73, 86; photo Charlotte Wan/*O.N.E.* (Oxfam News E-magazine – www.oxfam.org.hk/one): p. 65; photos Werner Forman Archive: pp. 44, 74; photo E. H. Wilson: p. 59; photo © Piero Zilio (www.pierozilio.eu/): p. 83.

# Index

*italic* numbers refer to illustrations; **bold** to recipes

adulteration 98

Aerated Bread Company (ABC) 106

Afghanistan 66, 67, 68, 71–2, *72*, 75

Africa 16

African teas 150, 153

afternoon tea 90, 103–4, *104*, 109, *109*, 111, 116, 117, 118, 122, 130, *131*, 131, 136, 144, 157

Afternoon tea blend 159

Algeria 82

apple tea 80

Abdulhamid (Sultan of the Ottoman Empire) 77

Assam 11, 12, 13, 16, 103, 127, 128, 130, 134, 137, 140, 143, 159, 161, 164

Assam Tea Company 128

Assam variety 12, 127, 130

Atatürk 78

*atkän çay* 70

Atkinson, Captain G. F. *132*

Australia 123–4

Bada, Yunnan 11

Bah Buton 143

*bambay chai* 71

*bancha* 48, 159, 160

Banks, Sir Joseph 126

barley tea 53

bed tea 131

Beeton, Mrs 149

Belmont, Frederick 109

Bettys Café Tea Rooms 109, *109*

Bhutan 126

Big Leaf 17

billy tea 123, *123*, 124

black tea 13, 15–16, 17, 20, 31, 39, 49, 54, 65, 70, 71, 81, 82, 88, 91, 98, 119, 122, 127, 128, 137, 143, 148, 152, 153, 159, 160, 161, 162, 163, 164

Blechynden, Richard 119

blending 16, 20, 21, 24

Bodhidharma 10, 42

Bohea 127, 159

*bo-jha* 59

Boston Tea Party 115, *115*

brick tea 28, 30, 46, 57, 59, 75
  see also tea bricks
Bruce, Robert 127
bubble tea 54, *55*, 56, 121
Burma 17, 28, 57, 58, 125
butter tea 59, 61, 125
Bützer, Fritz *see* Belmont,
  Frederick

caddy 45, *87*, *93*, 99
caffeine 48, 154
Cambodian variety 12
camel caravan 75, *75*, 148
*Camellia sinensis* 7, 10, *11*, 12,
  18, *51*, 127
Canada 122–3
caravan teas 159
caravanserais 66
'Carmontelle' *89*
Cassat, Mary, *The Cup of Tea*
  *116*
Catharine of Braganza 93
Catherine the Great 75
*çaydanlık* 79
Çelebi, Evliya 77
Ceylon, see also Sri Lanka 16,
  49, 81, 103, 119, 140, 142,
  143, 159, 160, 162
  Ceylon blend 142
  Ceylon teas 142
*Ch'a Ching* 28, 46
*cha kaiseki* 43
*chado* 42
*chai* (Indian) 63, 71, 133, 136,
  159
  *chaikhana* 66, *67*, 69, *69*
  *chai wallah* 132, 133, *134*

chai (American) 121, 159
*chaire* 45
*Chamada* 17, 57, 58
*Chamagudao* 17
*cha-no-y*, 14, 42, 43, 48
Charles II 93
*chasaku* 45
*chasen* 45
*chashitsu* 43
*chawan* 45
China 11, 13, 14, 15, 16, 18,
  24, 27–41, 46, 47, 52, 53,
  54, 57, 58, 72, 73, 74, 85, 94,
  96, 113, 126, 127, 128, 129,
  143, 146, 147, 148, 152,
  153, 159–64
china (porcelain) 87, *103*, 104,
  *105*, 148
China caravan 148
China tea 93, 98, 103, 107,
  125, 159, 160, 161
China variety 12
Chinese Tea Eggs **152–3**
Chinese tea plants 130
Chongan County 16
*chota hazri* 131
chrysanthemum 159
chun mee 39, 160
clipper ships 8, 94, *95*, 96
compressed teas 17
congou 160, 161
Countess of Boufflers-
  Rouverel *89*
Cranston, Kate 107
Cranston, Stuart 106
Crozier, Gladys 109–10
Cruikshank, Robert *100–1*

Cutchee tea 130

Da Ye 18
*dabal chai* 71
*dancha* 46
Darjeeling 13, 16, 88, 130, 131, 138, *138*, 140, 159, 160
*demlik* 79
Dengyo Daishi 46
Dharma 10
dim sum 38
Dimbula 142, 160
Dragon Well tea 39–41, 160
drying tea in China *17*
Duchess of Bedford 102
Dutch East India Company 143
Dutch tea drinking 86–7, *86*

Earl Grey 24, 103, 160, 163
East India Company 93, 94, 102, 113, 126, 127, 128
East Indiamen 94
Egypt 81, 84
Eisai 47
Eliza Acton's The Regent's or George The Fourth's Punch **151**
Emperor Huei Tsung 31
England 87, 91–112
English breakfast 160, 161
*Erh Ya* 27
Ezekiel, Nissim 135–6

Fauchon's Grand Salon de Thé *90*
Fedorovich, Mikhail (Tsar of Russia) 74
fermented tea 125
five o'clock tea 90
flavoured teas 24
flower tea *25*
flowering teas 26
Formosa 15, 53, 151 *see also* Taiwan
Fortune, Robert 128–30, *129*
France 87, 88–90, 91
French tea 90
Frederick the Great 88
Fu Baoshi, *Playing Weiqi at the Water Pavilion 33*
Fujian province 8, 13, 14, 54, 160, 162, 163

Gan Lu 11
Garraway, Thomas 91
*genmaicha* 48, 160
Georgia 75, 152
Germany 87–8
Gladstone, William 145
*Gong cha* 40
*gongfu* 15, 160
grading and blending 20–21, 24
Grand Oolong Fancy 54
Great China Tea Race 94, *95*
Great Tea Route 73
green tea 13, 14, 15, 20, 39, 41, 43, 46, 47, 48, 49, 51, 52, 54, 63, 65, 70, 71, 81, 85, 90, 91, 98, 112, 127, 140, 143, 148, 149, 150, 151, 152, 153
Green Tea Ice Cream **155–6**
Guanyin, the Iron Goddess of Mercy 15

*gulabi chai* 71
Gulf States 84
gunpowder 39, 161
Gunung Rosa 143
*gyokuro* 49, 51, 161

H. M. Blend 161
H'mong tea farmers
    (Vietnam) *65*
Hanway, Jonas 98
herbal teas 26
Heungdeok (King of Korea)
    52
high tea 106, 117
*hiki-cha* 46
*hojicha* 48
Horniman, John 98
    Horniman's Tea *97*
hotels *see* afternoon tea
hot tea 120, 122
Huang Jin Gui 15
Hudson Bay Company 122
Hyson 161

iced tea *119,* 119, 120, 122, **150**
Imperial tea 40, 161
India 9, 10, 11, 12, 16, 49, 58,
    61, 63, 66, 67, 81, 88, 96,
    119, 121, 125–40, 143, 145,
    148, 159, 162
India House 128
Indian tea 103, 106
Indian tea propaganda van *133*
Indonesia 143–4
Inglis, James 124
Iran 66, 67, 72, 75, 135 *see also*
    Persia

Irani cafes 135–6
Iraq 84
Irish Breakfast 161

Jalayir, Is'mail *73*
Japan 14, 28, 42–51, 53, 63,
    159, 162, 163
    tea ceremony 42–6, *44, 45*
jasmine tea 24, 65
Jasmine Tea Sorbet **156**
John Company 94
Johnson, Dr Samuel 98–9, *99*

*kahwa* 70
Kashmir 66, 70–71, 75
Keemun 16, 39, 161
Kenilworth 161
Kenya 161
Kim Taeryom 52
*Kissa ôrai* 47
*kissaten* 49
*Kitcha-Yojoki* 47
*koicha* 45
*kök çay* 70
kombucha 162
*konacha* 49
Korea 52–3
*Kuang Ya* 27
Kunming Tea Factory 19
Kuo P'o 27

Ladakh 61
Lady Grey 162
Lady Londonderry 162
Laos 58
Lapsang souchong 16, 39, 162,
    163

Lay Jee 162
Lemon and Rose Tea Jelly
  **154–5**
*lephet* 61–2, 125
  *lephet* tray *62*
liberty tea 114
Libya 82
Lipton teas 120, 121, *141*
Lipton, Thomas 141–2
Long Jing 39, *40*, 160, 162
lotus-flavoured tea 63, 65
Louis XIV 88
low tea 116
Lu Tong 7
Lu Yü 28–30, 46
Lyon's tea shop *108*
Lyons, Joseph 108

Mackintosh, Charles Rennie
  107
Mandelslo, Albert 125, 126
Mao Shan 162
Mariage Frères 90
*masala chai* 121, 134, 145, *159*
*matcha* 14, 43, 45, 47, 48, 51,
  162
maté 162
Meng Mountain, Sichuan 11
Menghai Tea Factory 18
*miang* 125
milk in tea 91
Miss Cranston's tea rooms
  107–8, *107*
Mongolia 39, 74
monkeys gathering tea *19*
Moroccan tea 81, *81, 82,*
  **149–50**

Morocco 68, 80–81
Moscow tea 78
Munmu (King of Korea) 52

National Trust 111
Nepal 58
Nilgiri teas 139, 162
nippies 108, *108*
*nok ch'a* 52
North America 112–22
*nun chai* 71
nursery teas, 104
Nuwara Eliya 142, 162

*O-chazuke* 51, **154**
Oolong tea 13, 14–15, 20, 39,
  54, 65, 71, 148, 150, 151,
  152, 153
Opium War 96
Orange Pekoe 21
Oriental beauty 54
Ovington, Reverend John
  125–6

*paani kum chai* 136
Pai Mu Tan 13
*pak-ho* 21
*Panyaro Sen* 52
Paraguay tea 163
pearl tea 150
*pek-ho* 21
Pekoe 21
Pepys, Samuel 91–3, *92*
Persia 72 *see also* Iran
pickled tea 125
pinhead gunpowder 161
pink tea 71

Pitt, William the Younger
  96
plucking tea on the
  Tregothnan Estate *112*
*po cha* 59
*pori ch'a* 53
pouchong 54, 163
Princess Wen Cheng 58
Puerh city 16, 17
Puerh teas 16–20, *21*, 39, 58,
  153

*qahwah* 70
*quan hong tra* 64
*qymaq chai* 71

Ramusio, Giambatista 85
red tea 15, 152
Rinjing Dorje 60–61, *60*
Rooibos 163
rose congou 149
Russell, Lillian 118–19
Russia 57, 73–7, 159
Russian caravan 159
Russian tea 77, 163

Saga (Emperor of Japan) 46
Saicho 46
Saint James tea 163
*salon(s) de Thé* 88, 90, *90*
samovar 69, 71, *73, 75–7, 76, 78,*
  *79,* 80
scented teas 24
Scotland 93
*sencha* 48, 163
Sen Rikyu 42–3
Sévigné, Madame de 91

*sheer chai* 71
Shen Nong (Emperor of
  China) 10
Shomu (Emperor of Japan) 46
Shrimps in Dragon Well Tea
  **153**
Shui Xian 15, 39
Shuko (Zen priest) 42
Sichuan 11, 16, 27, 32, 36, 37,
  41, 57, 58
Sichuan Imperial 16
Silk Road 28, 57, 58, 66–70
silver needles 13
smoky teas 16
smuggling 96
Sŏndŏk (Queen of Korea) 52
Song Ping cakes 18
Songstan Gambo (King of
  Tibet) 58
Souchong 163
South Africa 152
South America 16
South Silk Road 58
Spiced Tea **152**
Sri Lanka 13, 16, 88, 140–142,
  159, 160, 162, 164 *see also*
  Ceylon
Stamp Tax 113
Steel, Flora Annie 130
Sullivan, Thomas 120
sun tea 120
*syn çay* 70

*tach'on* 52
*tado* 53
Taiwan 15, 53–6, 121, 163, 164
  *see also* Formosa

Talon 143
tannin 49, 148
Taylor, James 140
    Taylor's of Harrogate 24,
    164
Tea Act 114
tea and health 146, *146*
tea and tango 109, *110*
tea as a flavouring 41, 51, 148,
    152–8
Tea Association of India 131,
    132
tea bags 120–21
Tea Board of Indonesia 143
tea bricks 20, 57, *59 see also*
    brick tea
tea bushes (in Nishio, Japan) *50*
tea caddy *see* caddy
tea ceremony
    Japan 42–6, *44, 45*
    Korea 53
    Mongolia *74*
tea chemistry 154
tea churn (s) *60*, 60, *61*
tea clippers *see* clipper ships
Tea Cup **151–2**
Tea Cup Trifle **158**
tea dances 109, 110, *110*, 118
tea doll 122, *122*
tea eggs 41
tea etymology 8
tea gardens 102, 113
tea house(s) 31, 32, *34–5, 36*,
    37, *37*, 38, 39, 49, 54, 66, 69,
    77, 80, 88 *see also chaikhana*
tea jelly 51, **154–5**
Tea Loaf **157**

tea nets 121
tea parties *100–1, 117*
tea pickers *137, 140, 139*
tea plantations of China *129*
tea receptions and 'At Homes'
    106
Tea Road 57, 73–5
tea rooms 45, 48, 77, *90*, 106,
    *107*, 107, 108, *109*, 111, 117,
    122
tea service *118*
tea shops 64, *64*, 108, *108*, 110,
    133
tea socks 121
tea tasters at work *24*
tea urn *93*
tea wagons 94
Tea Water Pump Garden 113
Tea-Horse Road 17, 28, 57, 58
tea-smoked duck 41
tea-tasting terms 22–3
*tencha* 49
Tetleys 121
Thailand 65–6, 125
*Thé Dansant* 109, 119
*Thé l'Opéra* 90
*Thea assamica* 12
theanine 154
Tibet 17, 28, 39, 57, 58–61, 124
Tie Guan Yin 15
tiffin 130, 136
tippy teas 137
tisanes 26
To Make Tea **149**
*tôcha* 47
Todonai, Robert, *Stockmen's
    Rest 124*

Tregothnan Estate 112, *112*
Trench, Richard *68*
tuancha 19
Tuareg tea 81, *83*
Tu Duc (King of Vietnam) 63
Tu Hsiao Shan 30–31
Tung Ting 54, 164
Tunisia 82
tuocha 20
Turkey 75, 77–80, *79*
   Turkish tea *80*
Twankey 164
Twinings 24
Tyumenets 74

Üisun 53
United Kingdom Tea
   Company *90*
United States 112–22
*usucha* 45

van Linschoten, Jan Huyghen
   85
Verkolje, Nicolaes *86*
Vietnam 58, 63–5, *64*

Welsh Brew 164
whisked green tea, Korea *52*
white peony 13
White Rose Redi-Tea 120
white tea 13, 31, 65
Willow Tea Rooms 108
WRVS serving tea *111*

Xishuangbanna 17

yellow tea 13–14

Yin Zhen 13
Yixing teapot(s) 31, *32, 33*, 161
Yorkshire tea 24, 164
Yoshimasa 48
Young Hyson 161
*yum cha* 38
Yunnan 11, 16, 17, 26, 57, 58,
   164

Zen Buddhists 31
Zhen Wu Li 11
Zulu tea 164